# Microsoft® Official Academic Course

# Software Development Fundamentals, Exam 98-361

WILEY

# Credits

| | |
|---|---|
| EDITOR | Bryan Gambrel |
| DIRECTOR OF SALES | Mitchell Beaton |
| EXECUTIVE MARKETING MANAGER | Chris Ruel |
| MICROSOFT SENIOR PRODUCT MANAGER | Merrick Van Dongen of Microsoft Learning |
| EDITORIAL PROGRAM ASSISTANT | Jennifer Lartz |
| CONTENT MANAGER | Micheline Frederick |
| PRODUCTION EDITOR | Amy Weintraub |
| CREATIVE DIRECTOR | Harry Nolan |
| COVER DESIGNER | Jim O'Shea |
| TECHNOLOGY AND MEDIA | Tom Kulesa/Wendy Ashenberg |

Cover photo: Credit: © Pgiam/iStockphoto

This book was set in Garamond by Aptara, Inc. and printed and bound by Bind Rite Robbinsville.
The cover was printed by Bind Rite Robbinsville.

Founded in 1807, John Wiley & Sons, Inc. has been a valued source of knowledge and understanding for more than 200 years, helping people around the world meet their needs and fulfill their aspirations. Our company is built on a foundation of principles that include responsibility to the communities we serve and where we live and work. In 2008, we launched a Corporate Citizenship Initiative, a global effort to address the environmental, social, economic, and ethical challenges we face in our business. Among the issues we are addressing are carbon impact, paper specifications and procurement, ethical conduct within our business and among our vendors, and community and charitable support. For more information, please visit our website: www.wiley.com/go/citizenship.

ISBN 978-0-470-88911-4

Printed in the United States of America

10 9 8 7 6 5 4 3 2 1

# Foreword from the Publisher

Wiley's publishing vision for the Microsoft Official Academic Course series is to provide students and instructors with the skills and knowledge they need to use Microsoft technology effectively in all aspects of their personal and professional lives. Quality instruction is required to help both educators and students get the most from Microsoft's software tools and to become more productive. Thus our mission is to make our instructional programs trusted educational companions for life.

To accomplish this mission, Wiley and Microsoft have partnered to develop the highest quality educational programs for Information Workers, IT Professionals, and Developers. Materials created by this partnership carry the brand name "Microsoft Official Academic Course," assuring instructors and students alike that the content of these textbooks is fully endorsed by Microsoft, and that they provide the highest quality information and instruction on Microsoft products. The Microsoft Official Academic Course textbooks are "Official" in still one more way—they are the officially sanctioned courseware for Microsoft IT Academy members.

The Microsoft Official Academic Course series focuses on *workforce development*. These programs are aimed at those students seeking to enter the workforce, change jobs, or embark on new careers as information workers, IT professionals, and developers. Microsoft Official Academic Course programs address their needs by emphasizing authentic workplace scenarios with an abundance of projects, exercises, cases, and assessments.

The Microsoft Official Academic Courses are mapped to Microsoft's extensive research and job-task analysis, the same research and analysis used to create the Microsoft Technology Associate (MTA) and Microsoft Certified Information Technology Professional (MCITP) exams. The textbooks focus on real skills for real jobs. As students work through the projects and exercises in the textbooks, they enhance their level of knowledge and their ability to apply the latest Microsoft technology to everyday tasks. These students also gain resume-building credentials that can assist them in finding a job, keeping their current job, or in furthering their education.

The concept of life-long learning is today an utmost necessity. Job roles, and even whole job categories, are changing so quickly that none of us can stay competitive and productive without continuously updating our skills and capabilities. The Microsoft Official Academic Course offerings, and their focus on Microsoft certification exam preparation, provide a means for people to acquire and effectively update their skills and knowledge. Wiley supports students in this endeavor through the development and distribution of these courses as Microsoft's official academic publisher.

Today educational publishing requires attention to providing quality print and robust electronic content. By integrating Microsoft Official Academic Course products, *WileyPLUS*, and Microsoft certifications, we are better able to deliver efficient learning solutions for students and teachers alike.

**Bonnie Lieberman**

General Manager and Senior Vice President

# Preface

Welcome to the Microsoft Official Academic Course (MOAC) program for Software Development Fundamentals. MOAC represents the collaboration between Microsoft Learning and John Wiley & Sons, Inc. publishing company. Microsoft and Wiley teamed up to produce a series of textbooks that deliver compelling and innovative teaching solutions to instructors and superior learning experiences for students. Infused and informed by in-depth knowledge from the creators of Microsoft products, and crafted by a publisher known world-wide for the pedagogical quality of its products, these textbooks maximize skills transfer in minimum time. Students are challenged to reach their potential by using their new technical skills as highly productive members of the workforce.

Because this knowledge base comes directly from Microsoft, creator of the Microsoft Certified Technology Specialist (MCTS), Microsoft Certified Professional (MCP), and Microsoft Technology Associate (MTA) exams (www.microsoft.com/learning/certification), you are sure to receive the topical coverage that is most relevant to your personal and professional success. Microsoft's direct participation not only assures you that MOAC textbook content is accurate and current; it also means that you will receive the best instruction possible to enable your success on certification exams and in the workplace.

## ■ The Microsoft Official Academic Course Program

The *Microsoft Official Academic Course* series is a complete program for instructors and institutions to prepare and deliver great courses on Microsoft software technologies. With MOAC, we recognize that, because of the rapid pace of change in the technology and curriculum developed by Microsoft, there is an ongoing set of needs beyond classroom instruction tools for an instructor to be ready to teach the course. The MOAC program endeavors to provide solutions for all these needs in a systematic manner in order to ensure a successful and rewarding course experience for both instructor and student—technical and curriculum training for instructor readiness with new software releases; the software itself for student use at home for building hands-on skills, assessment, and validation of skill development; and a great set of tools for delivering instruction in the classroom and lab. All are important to the smooth delivery of an interesting course on Microsoft software, and all are provided with the MOAC program. We think about the model below as a gauge for ensuring that we completely support you in your goal of teaching a great course. As you evaluate your instructional materials options, you may wish to use this model for comparison purposes with available products:

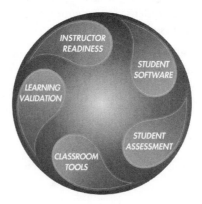

**www.wiley.com/college/microsoft or
call the MOAC Toll-Free Number: 1+(888) 764-7001 (U.S. & Canada only)**

## ▪ Pedagogical Features

The MOAC textbook for Software Development Fundamentals is designed to cover all the learning objectives for that MTA exam 98-361, which is referred to as its "exam objective." The Microsoft Technology Associate (MTA) exam objectives are highlighted throughout the textbook. Many pedagogical features have been developed specifically for the *Microsoft Official Academic Course* program.

Presenting the extensive procedural information and technical concepts woven throughout the textbook raises challenges for the student and instructor alike. The Illustrated Book Tour that follows provides a guide to the rich features contributing to the *Microsoft Official Academic Course* program's pedagogical plan. The following is a list of key features in each lesson designed to prepare students for success as they continue in their IT education, on the certification exams, and in the workplace:

- Each lesson begins with a **Lesson Skill Matrix**. More than a standard list of learning objectives, the Lesson Skill Matrix correlates each software skill covered in the lesson to the specific exam objective.

- Concise and frequent **step-by-step** Exercises teach students new features and provide an opportunity for hands-on practice. Numbered steps give detailed, step-by-step instructions to help students learn software skills.

- **Illustrations**—in particular, screen images—provide visual feedback as students work through the exercises. The images reinforce key concepts, provide visual clues about the steps, and allow students to check their progress.

- Lists of **Key Terms** at the beginning of each lesson introduce students to important technical vocabulary. When these terms are used later in the lesson, they appear in bold italic type where they are defined.

- Engaging point-of-use **Reader Aids**, located throughout the lessons, tell students why this topic is relevant (*The Bottom Line*), provide students with helpful hints (*Take Note*). Reader Aids also provide additional relevant or background information that adds value to the lesson.

- **Certification Ready** features throughout the text signal students where a specific certification objective is covered. They provide students with a chance to check their understanding of that particular MTA objective and, if necessary, review the section of the lesson where it is covered. MOAC offers complete preparation for MTA certification.

- **End-of-Lesson Questions:** The Knowledge Assessment section provides a variety of multiple-choice, true-false, matching, and fill-in-the-blank questions.

- **End-of-Lesson Exercises:** Competency Assessment case scenarios, Proficiency Assessment case scenarios, and Workplace Ready exercises are projects that test students' ability to apply what they've learned in the lesson.

# ■ Lesson Features

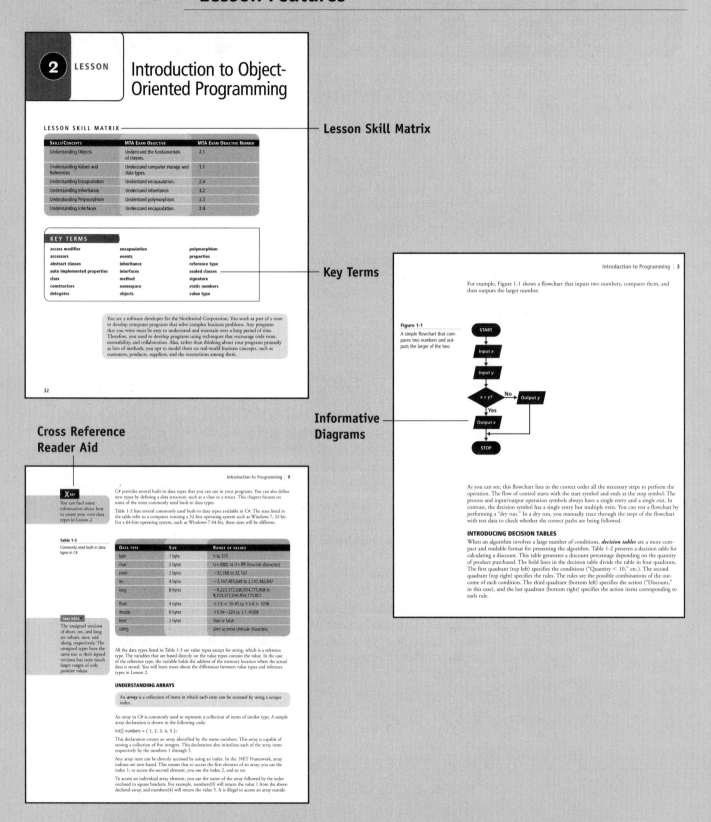

**Lesson Skill Matrix**

**Key Terms**

**Informative Diagrams**

**Cross Reference Reader Aid**

44 | Lesson 2

2. Modify the code of the Program class to the following:

```
class Program
{
    static void Main(string[] args)
    {
        Rectangle rect = new Rectangle
            { Length = 10.0, Width = 20.0 };
        Console.WriteLine("Shape Name: {0}, Area: {1}",
            Rectangle.ShapeName,
            rect.GetArea());
    }
}
```

3. Select **Debug > Start Without Debugging**. A console window will pop up to display the name and area of the shape.
4. SAVE your project.

**PAUSE.** Leave the project open to use in the next exercise.

When an instance of a class is created, a separate copy is created for each instance field, but only one copy of a static field is shared by all instances.

A static member cannot be referenced through an instance object. Instead, a static member is referenced through the class name (such as Rectangle.ShapeName in the above exercise). Note that it is not possible to use the *this* keyword reference with a static method or property because the *this* keyword can only be used to access instance objects.

**CERTIFICATION READY**
Do you understand the fundamentals of classes?
2.1

### Understanding Values and References

THE BOTTOM LINE — A value type directly stores a value, whereas a reference type only stores a reference to an actual value.

A *value type* directly stores data within its memory. *Reference types*, on the other hand, store only a reference to a memory location; here, the actual data is stored at the memory location being referred to. Most built-in elementary data types (such as bool, int, char, double, etc.) are value types. User-defined data types created by using the keyword struct are value types as well. Reference types include the types created by using the keywords object, string, interface, delegate, and class.

#### Understanding Structs

> The keyword *struct* is used to create user-defined types that consist of small groups of related fields. Structs are value types—as opposed to classes, which are reference types.

Structs are defined by using the keyword struct, as shown below:

```
public struct Point
{
    public double X, Y;
}
```

Structs can contain most of the elements that classes can contain, such as constructors, methods, properties, etc. However, as you'll learn in the next section, structs are value types,

**The Bottom Line Reader Aid**

---

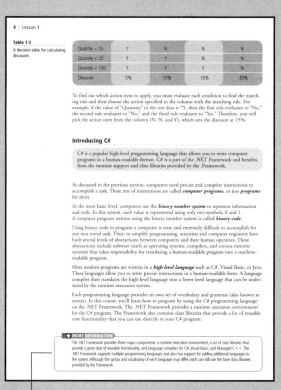

4 | Lesson 1

**Table 1-2**
A decision table for calculating discounts

| Quantity < 10 | Y | N | N | N |
| Quantity < 50 | Y | Y | N | N |
| Quantity < 100 | Y | Y | Y | N |
| Discount | 5% | 10% | 15% | 20% |

To find out which action item to apply, you must evaluate each condition to find the matching rule and then choose the action specified in the column with the matching rule. For example, if the value of "Quantity" in the test data is 75, then the first rule evaluates to "No," the second rule evaluates to "No," and the third rule evaluates to "Yes." Therefore, you will pick the action item from the column (N, N, and Y), which sets the discount at 15%.

#### Introducing C#

> C# is a popular high-level programming language that allows you to write computer programs in a human-readable format. C# is a part of the .NET Framework and benefits from the runtime support and class libraries provided by the .Framework.

As discussed in the previous section, computers need precise and complete instructions to accomplish a task. These sets of instructions are called *computer programs*, or just *programs* for short.

At the most basic level, computers use the *binary number system* to represent information and code. In this system, each value is represented using only two symbols, 0 and 1. A computer program written using the binary number system is called *binary code*.

Using binary code to program a computer is terse and extremely difficult to accomplish for any non trivial task. Thus, to simplify programming, scientists and computer engineers have built several levels of abstractions between computers and their human operators. These abstractions include software (such as operating systems, compilers, and various runtime systems) that takes responsibility for translating a human-readable program into a machine-readable program.

Most modern programs are written in a *high-level language* such as C#, Visual Basic, or Java. These languages allow you to write precise instructions in a human-readable form. A language compiler then translates the high-level language into a lower-level language that can be understood by the runtime execution system.

Each programming language provides its own set of vocabulary and grammar (also known as syntax). In this course, you'll learn how to program by using the C# programming language on the .NET Framework. The .NET Framework provides a runtime execution environment for the C# program. The Framework also contains class libraries that provide a lot of reusable core functionality that you can use directly in your C# program.

**MORE INFORMATION**
The .NET Framework provides three major components: a runtime execution environment, a set of class libraries that provide a great deal of reusable functionality, and language compilers for C#, Visual Basic, and Managed C++. The .NET Framework supports multiple programming languages and also has support for adding additional languages to the system. Although the syntax and vocabulary of each language may differ, each can still use the base class libraries provided by the Framework.

**More information Reader Aid**

---

Understanding General Software Development | 77

BubbleSort works by comparing two elements to check whether they are out of order; if they are, it swaps them. The algorithm continues to do this until the entire list is in the desired order. BubbleSort gets its name from the way the algorithm works: As the algorithm progresses, the smaller items are "bubbled" up.

Let's visualize BubbleSort with the help of an example. Say you want to arrange all the items in the following list in ascending order: (20, 30, 10, 40). These items should be arranged from smallest to largest. The BubbleSort algorithm attempts to solve this problem in one or more passes, with each pass completely scanning the list of items. If the algorithm encounters out-of-order elements, it swaps them. The algorithm finishes when it scans the whole list without swapping any elements. If there are no swaps, then none of the elements were out of order and the list has been completely sorted.

**Table 3-1**
BubbleSort first pass

| STEP | BEFORE | AFTER | COMMENTS |
|------|--------|-------|----------|
| 1 | 20, 30, 10, 40 | 20, 30, 10, 40 | The algorithm compares the first two elements (20 and 30); because they are in the correct order, no swap is needed. |
| 2 | 20, 30, 10, 40 | 20, 10, 30, 40 | The algorithm compares the next two elements (30 and 10); because they are out of order, the elements are swapped. |
| 3 | 20, 10, 30, 40 | 20, 10, 30, 40 | The algorithm compares the next two elements (30 and 40); because they are in the correct order, no swap is needed. |

As shown in Table 3-1, at the end of first pass, BubbleSort has performed one swap, and there is the possibility that the items are not yet completely sorted. Therefore, BubbleSort gives the list another pass, as depicted in Table 3-2.

**Table 3-2**
BubbleSort second pass

| STEP | BEFORE | AFTER | COMMENTS |
|------|--------|-------|----------|
| 1 | 20, 10, 30, 40 | 10, 20, 30, 40 | The algorithm compares the first two elements (20 and 10); because they are out of order, the elements are swapped. |
| 2 | 10, 20, 30, 40 | 10, 20, 30, 40 | The algorithm compares the next two elements (20 and 30); because they are in the correct order, no swap is needed. |
| 3 | 10, 20, 30, 40 | 10, 20, 30, 40 | The algorithm compares the next two elements (30 and 40); because they are in the correct order, no swap is needed. |

**Easy-to-Read Tables**

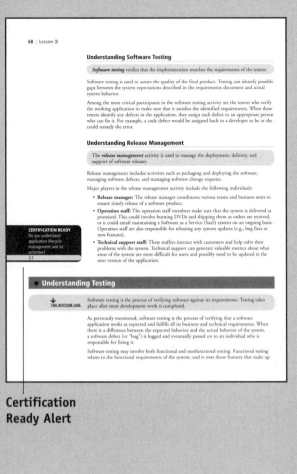

**Certification
Ready Alert**

**Step-by-Step Exercises**

**Take Note
Reader Aid**

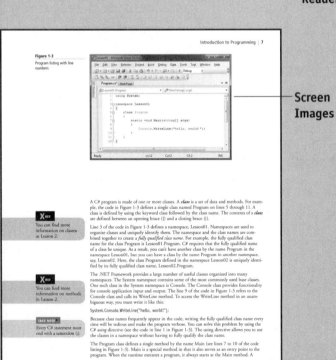

**Screen
Images**

**Take Note Reader Aid**

Understanding General Software Development | 69

the core functionality of the system. For example, testing whether users can add items to a shopping cart is an important part of functional testing for an e-commerce Web site. In comparison, nonfunctional testing involves testing software attributes that are not part of the core functionality but rather part of the software's nonfunctional requirements, such as scalability, usability, security.

 **TAKE NOTE** It is important to note that the process of software testing can only *help* find defects—it cannot guarantee the absence of defects. Complex software has a huge number of possible execution paths and many parameters that can affect its behavior. It is not feasible and often not possible to test all the different situations that such software will encounter in a production environment.

### Understanding Testing Methods

Software testing *methods* are generally divided into two categories: white-box and black-box testing.

Traditionally, there are two broad approaches to software testing:

- **Black-box testing**
- **White-box testing**

Black-box testing treats the software as a black box, focusing solely on inputs and outputs. With this approach, any knowledge of internal system workings is not used during testing. In contrast, with white-box testing, testers use their knowledge of system internals when testing the system. For example, in white-box testing, the testers have access to the source code.

These two testing techniques complement each other. Black-box testing is mostly used to make sure a software application covers all its requirements. Meanwhile, white-box testing is used to make sure that each method or function has proper test cases available.

### Understanding Testing Levels

Testing is performed at various phases of the application development lifecycle. Different *testing levels* specify where in the lifecycle a particular test takes place, as well as what kind of test is being performed.

Testing levels are defined by where the testing takes place within the course of the software development lifecycle. Five distinct levels of testing exist:

- **Unit testing:** Unit testing verifies the functionality of a unit of code. For example, a unit test may assess whether a method returns the correct value. Unit testing is white-box testing, and it is frequently done by the developer who is writing the code. Unit testing often uses an automated tool that can simplify the development of cases and also keep track of whether a code modification causes any of the existing unit tests to fail. Visual Studio has built-in support for unit testing. You can also use open-source tools such as NUnit to automate unit tests for the .NET Framework code.
- **Integration testing:** Integration testing assesses the interface between software components. Integration testing can be performed incrementally as the components are being

---

**Skill Summary**

Understanding Databases | 173

### SKILL SUMMARY

**IN THIS LESSON, YOU LEARNED THE FOLLOWING:**

- A relational database organizes information into tables. A table is a list of rows and columns.
- Relational database design is the process of determining the appropriate relational database structure to satisfy the business requirements.
- Entity-relationship diagrams are used to model the entities, their attributes, and the relationships among entities. The entity-relationship diagrams can help you in determine what data needs to be stored in a database.
- The process of data normalization ensures that a database design is free of any problems that could lead to loss of data integrity. Most design issues can be resolved by ensuring that the tables satisfy the requirements of the third normal form.
- The Structured Query Language (SQL) provides statements such as SELECT, INSERT, UPDATE, and DELETE to work with relational data.
- A stored procedure is a set of SQL statements that is stored in a database. Stored procedures can be used by multiple applications.
- The XmlReader and XmlWriter classes provide a fast, noncached, forward-only way to read or write XML data. The XmlDocument class is an in-memory representation of XML data and allows navigation and editing of the XML document.
- The DataSet class represents an in-memory representation of relational data. The DataAdapter class acts as a bridge between the data source and the DataSet. The DataAdapter stores the data connection and data commands needed to connect to the data source.

**Knowledge Assessment**

### ■ Knowledge Assessment

**Fill in the Blank**

*Complete the following sentences by writing the correct word or words in the blanks provided.*

1. In order for a table to be in the _____, none of the columns should have multiple values in the same row of data.
2. The _____ requires that all non-key columns are functionally dependent on the entire primary key.
3. The _____ requires that there is no functional dependency among non-key attributes.
4. The basic building blocks for an entity-relationship diagram are _____, _____, and _____.
5. The _____ clause in a SELECT statement evaluates each row for a condition and decides whether to include it in the result set.
6. The object used with the *using* statement must implement the _____ interface.
7. T-SQL's _____ statement can be used to create a stored procedure.

---

64 | Lesson 2

### ■ Competency Assessment

**Scenario 2-1: Creating Properties**

You need to create a class named Product that represents a product. The class has a single property named Name. Users of the Product class should be able to get as well as set the value of the Name property. However, any attempt to set the value of Name to an empty string or a null value should raise an exception. Also, users of the Product class should not be able to access any other data members of the Product class. How will you create such a class?

**Scenario 2-2: Creating a Struct**

You are developing a game that needs to represent the location of a target in three-dimensional space. The location is identified by the three integer values denoted x, y, and z. You will create thousands of these data structures in your program, and you need a lightweight, efficient way to store this data in memory. Also, it is unlikely that you will need to inherit any other types from this location type. How should you represent the location in your program?

### ■ Proficiency Assessment

**Scenario 2-1: Overriding the ToString Method**

Say you are writing code for a Product class. The Product class contains the name and price of a product. You need to override the base class (System.Object) method ToString to provide information about the objects of the product class to the calling code. What code do you need to write for the Product class in order to meet this requirement?

**Scenario 2-2: Creating and Handling Events** — **Case Scenarios**

Imagine that you are writing code for creating and handling events in your program. The class SampleClass needs to implement the following interface:

```
public delegate void SampleDelegate();
public interface ISampleEvents
{
    event SampleDelegate SampleEvent;
    void Invoke();
}
```

You need to write code for the SampleClass and for a test method that creates an instance of the SampleClass and invokes the event. What code should you write?

---

# Conventions and Features Used in This Book

This book uses particular fonts, symbols, and heading conventions to highlight important information or to call your attention to special steps. For more information about the features in each lesson, refer to the Illustrated Book Tour section.

| CONVENTION | MEANING |
|---|---|
| ↓ THE BOTTOM LINE | This feature provides a brief summary of the material to be covered in the section that follows. |
| CERTIFICATION READY | This feature signals the point in the text where a specific certification objective is covered. It provides you with a chance to check your understanding of that particular MTA objective and, if necessary, review the section of the lesson where it is covered. |
| TAKE NOTE* | Reader Aids appear in shaded boxes found in your text. *Take Note* provides helpful hints related to particular tasks or topics. |
| X REF | These notes provide pointers to information discussed elsewhere in the textbook or describe interesting features that are not directly addressed in the current topic or exercise. |
| Alt + Tab | A plus sign (+) between two key names means that you must press both keys at the same time. Keys that you are instructed to press in an exercise will appear in the font shown here. |
| *Example* | Key terms appear in bold italic when they are defined. |

# Instructor Support Program

The *Microsoft Official Academic Course* programs are accompanied by a rich array of resources that incorporate the extensive textbook visuals to form a pedagogically cohesive package. These resources provide all the materials instructors need to deploy and deliver their courses. Resources available online for download include:

- The **MSDN Academic Alliance** is designed to provide the easiest and most inexpensive developer tools, products, and technologies available to faculty and students in labs, classrooms, and on student PCs. A free three-year membership is available to qualified MOAC adopters.

  *Note:* Microsoft Windows 2008 Server, Microsoft Windows 7, and Microsoft Visual Studio can be downloaded from MSDN AA for use by students in this course.

- The **Instructor's Guide** contains solutions to all the textbook exercises and syllabi for various term lengths. The Instructor's Guide also includes chapter summaries and lecture notes. The Instructor's Guide is available from the Book Companion site (http://www.wiley.com/college/microsoft).

- The **Test Bank** contains hundreds of questions in multiple-choice, true-false, short answer, and essay formats, and is available to download from the Instructor's Book Companion site (www.wiley.com/college/microsoft). A complete answer key is provided.

- A complete set of **PowerPoint presentations and images** are available on the Instructor's Book Companion site (http://www.wiley.com/college/microsoft) to enhance classroom presentations. Approximately 50 PowerPoint slides are provided for each lesson. Tailored to the text's topical coverage and Skills Matrix, these presentations are designed to convey key concepts addressed in the text. All images from the text are on the Instructor's Book Companion site (http://www.wiley.com/college/microsoft). You can incorporate them into your PowerPoint presentations, or create your own overhead transparencies and handouts. By using these visuals in class discussions, you can help focus students' attention on key elements of technologies covered and help them understand how to use it effectively in the workplace.

- When it comes to improving the classroom experience, there is no better source of ideas and inspiration than your fellow colleagues. The **Wiley Faculty Network** connects teachers with technology, facilitates the exchange of best practices, and helps to enhance instructional efficiency and effectiveness. Faculty Network activities include technology training and tutorials, virtual seminars, peer-to-peer exchanges of experiences and ideas, personal consulting, and sharing of resources. For details visit www.WhereFacultyConnect.com.

## MSDN ACADEMIC ALLIANCE—FREE 3-YEAR MEMBERSHIP AVAILABLE TO QUALIFIED ADOPTERS!

The Microsoft Developer Network Academic Alliance (MSDN AA) is designed to provide the easiest and most inexpensive way for universities to make the latest Microsoft developer tools, products, and technologies available in labs, classrooms, and on student PCs. MSDN AA is an annual membership program for departments teaching Science, Technology, Engineering, and Mathematics (STEM) courses. The membership provides a complete solution to keep academic labs, faculty, and students on the leading edge of technology.

Software available in the MSDN AA program is provided at no charge to adopting departments through the Wiley and Microsoft publishing partnership.

**As a bonus to this free offer, faculty will be introduced to Microsoft's Faculty Connection and Academic Resource Center. It takes time and preparation to keep students engaged while giving them a fundamental understanding of theory, and the Microsoft Faculty Connection is designed to help STEM professors with this preparation by providing articles, curriculum, and tools that professors can use to engage and inspire today's technology students.**

*Contact your Wiley representative for details.

For more information about the MSDN Academic Alliance program, go to:

**http://msdn.microsoft.com/academic/**

*Note:* Microsoft Windows Server 2008, Microsoft Windows 7, and Microsoft Visual Studio can be downloaded from MSDN AA for use by students in this course.

## ▪ Important Web Addresses and Phone Numbers

**To locate the Wiley Higher Education Rep in your area, go to http://www.wiley.com/college and click on the *"Who's My Rep?"* link at the top of the page, or call the MOAC Toll-Free Number: 1 + (888) 764-7001 (U.S. & Canada only).**

To learn more about becoming a Microsoft Certified Technology Specialist and exam availability, visit www.microsoft.com/learning/mcp/mcp.

# Student Support Program

## ■ Additional Resources

### Book Companion Web Site (www.wiley.com/college/microsoft)

The students' book companion Web site for the MOAC series includes any resources, exercise files, and Web links that will be used in conjunction with this course.

### Wiley Desktop Editions

Wiley MOAC Desktop Editions are innovative, electronic versions of printed textbooks. Students buy the desktop version for up to 50% off the U.S. price of the printed text, and they get the added value of permanence and portability. Wiley Desktop Editions provide students with numerous additional benefits that are not available with other e-text solutions.

Wiley Desktop Editions are NOT subscriptions; students download the Wiley Desktop Edition to their computer desktops. Students own the content they buy to keep for as long as they want. Once a Wiley Desktop Edition is downloaded to the computer desktop, students have instant access to all of the content without being online. Students can print the sections they prefer to read in hard copy. Students also have access to fully integrated resources within their Wiley Desktop Edition. From highlighting their e-text to taking and sharing notes, students can easily personalize their Wiley Desktop Edition as they are reading or following along in class.

## ■ About the Microsoft Technology Associate (MTA) Certification

### Preparing Tomorrow's Technology Workforce

Technology plays a role in virtually every business around the world. Possessing the fundamental knowledge of how technology works and understanding its impact on today's academic and workplace environment is increasingly important—particularly for students interested in exploring professions involving technology. That's why Microsoft created the Microsoft Technology Associate (MTA) certification—a new entry-level credential that validates fundamental technology knowledge among students seeking to build a career in technology.

The Microsoft Technology Associate (MTA) certification is the ideal and preferred path to Microsoft's world-renowned technology certification programs, such as Microsoft Certified Technology Specialist (MCTS) and Microsoft Certified IT Professional (MCITP). MTA is positioned to become the premier credential for individuals seeking to explore and pursue a career in technology, or augment related pursuits such as business or any other field where technology is pervasive.

## MTA Candidate Profile

The MTA certification program is designed specifically for secondary and post-secondary students interested in exploring academic and career options in a technology field. It offers students a certification in basic IT and development. As the new recommended entry point for Microsoft technology certifications, MTA is designed especially for students new to IT and software development. It is available exclusively in educational settings and easily integrates into the curricula of existing computer classes.

## MTA Empowers Educators and Motivates Students

MTA provides a new standard for measuring and validating fundamental technology knowledge right in the classroom while keeping your budget and teaching resources intact. MTA helps institutions stand out as innovative providers of high-demand industry credentials and is easily deployed with a simple, convenient, and affordable suite of entry-level technology certification exams. MTA enables students to explore career paths in technology without requiring a big investment of time and resources, while providing a career foundation and the confidence to succeed in advanced studies and future vocational endeavors.

In addition to giving students an entry-level Microsoft certification, MTA is designed to be a stepping stone to other, more advanced Microsoft technology certifications, like the Microsoft Certified Technology Specialist (MCTS) certification.

## Delivering MTA Exams: The MTA Campus License

Implementing a new certification program in your classroom has never been so easy with the MTA Campus License. Through the one-time purchase of the 12-month, 1,000-exam MTA Campus License, there's no more need for ad hoc budget requests and recurrent purchases of exam vouchers. Now you can budget for one low cost for the entire year, and then administer MTA exams to your students and other faculty across your entire campus where and when you want.

The MTA Campus License provides a convenient and affordable suite of entry-level technology certifications designed to empower educators and motivate students as they build a foundation for their careers.

The MTA Campus License is administered by Certiport, Microsoft's exclusive MTA exam provider.

To learn more about becoming a Microsoft Technology Associate and exam availability, visit www.microsoft.com/learning/mta.

# ■ Activate Your FREE MTA Practice Test!

Your purchase of this book entitles you to a free MTA practice test from GMetrix (a $30 value). Please go to www.gmetrix.com/mtatests and use the following validation code to redeem your free test: **MTA98-361-A19875B7D810**

The **GMetrix Skills Management System** provides everything you need to practice for the Microsoft Technology Associate (MTA) Certification.

Overview of Test features:

- Practice tests map to the Microsoft Technology Associate (MTA) exam objectives
- GMetrix MTA practice tests simulate the actual MTA testing environment
- 50+ questions per test covering all objectives
- Progress at own pace, save test to resume later, return to skipped questions
- Detailed, printable score report highlighting areas requiring further review

To get the most from your MTA preparation, take advantage of your free GMetrix MTA Practice Test today!

For technical support issues on installation or code activation, please email support@gmetrix.com.

# Acknowledgments

## ■ MOAC MTA Technology Fundamentals Reviewers

We'd like to thank the many reviewers who pored over the manuscript and provided invaluable feedback in the service of quality instructional materials:

Yuke Wang, University of Texas at Dallas

Palaniappan Vairavan, Bellevue College

Harold "Buz" Lamson, ITT Technical Institute

Colin Archibald, Valencia Community College

Catherine Bradfield, DeVry University Online

Robert Nelson, Blinn College

Kalpana Viswanathan, Bellevue College

Bob Becker, Vatterott College

Carol Torkko, Bellevue College

Bharat Kandel, Missouri Tech

Linda Cohen, Forsyth Technical Community College

Candice Lambert, Metro Technology Centers

Susan Mahon, Collin College

Mark Aruda, Hillsborough Community College

Claude Russo, Brevard Community College

David Koppy, Baker College

Sharon Moran, Hillsborough Community College

Keith Hoell, Briarcliffe College and Queens College— CUNY

Mark Hufnagel, Lee County School District

Rachelle Hall, Glendale Community College

Scott Elliott, Christie Digital Systems, Inc.

Gralan Gilliam, Kaplan

Steve Strom, Butler Community College

John Crowley, Bucks County Community College

Margaret Leary, Northern Virginia Community College

Sue Miner, Lehigh Carbon Community College

Gary Rollinson, Cabrillo College

Al Kelly, University of Advancing Technology

Katherine James, Seneca College

www.wiley.com/college/microsoft *or*
call the MOAC Toll-Free Number: 1+(888) 764-7001 (U.S. & Canada only)

# Brief Contents

# Contents

www.wiley.com/college/microsoft *or*
call the MOAC Toll-Free Number: 1+(888) 764-7001 (U.S. & Canada only)

# Introduction to Programming

## LESSON SKILL MATRIX

| SKILLS/CONCEPTS | MTA EXAM OBJECTIVE | MTA EXAM OBJECTIVE NUMBER |
| --- | --- | --- |
| Understanding Computer Programming | Understand computer storage and data types. | 1.1 |
| Understanding Decision Structures | Understand computer decision structures. | 1.2 |
| Understanding Repetition Structures | Identify the appropriate method for handling repetition. | 1.3 |
| Understanding Exception Handling | Understand error handling. | 1.4 |

## KEY TERMS

| | | |
| --- | --- | --- |
| algorithm | decision structures | if statement |
| array | decision table | if-else statement |
| binary code | default statement | methods |
| binary number system | do-while loop | operator |
| case | exception | recursion |
| class | finally block | switch block |
| computer programs (programs) | flowchart | switch statement |
| constant | for loop | try-catch-finally block |
| data types | foreach loop | variable |
| | high-level language | while loop |

Imagine that you are a software developer for the Northwind Corporation. As part of your job, you develop computer programs to solve business problems. Examples of the work you do include analyzing customer orders to determine applicable discounts, updating stock information for thousands of items in a company's inventory, and writing interactive reports that allow users to sort and filter data.

It is important for you to make sure your programs are designed exactly according to specifications. You also need to ensure that all computations are accurate and complete. The programs that you write need to be robust, and they should be able to display error messages but continue processing.

The programming language that you use provides you with various tools and techniques to get your tasks done. Based on the task at hand, you select the data types and the control structures that are best suited for solving the problem.

# ■ Understanding Computer Programming

THE BOTTOM LINE

A computer program is a set of precise instructions to complete a task. In this section, you'll learn how to write algorithms and computer programs to solve a given problem. In addition to writing your first computer program using the C# programming language, you'll also learn about the basic structure of computer programs and how to compile, execute, provide input to, and generate output from a program.

## Introducing Algorithms

An algorithm is a set of ordered and finite steps to solve a given problem.

The term *algorithm* refers to a method for solving problems. Algorithms can be described in English, but such descriptions are often misinterpreted because of the inherent complexity and ambiguity in a natural language. Hence, algorithms are frequently written in simple and more precise formats, such as flowcharts, decision trees, and decision tables, which represent an algorithm as a diagram, table, or graph. These techniques are often employed prior to writing programs in order to gain a better understanding of the solution.

These algorithm-development tools might help you in expressing a solution in an easy-to-use way, but they can't be directly understood by a computer. In order for a computer to understand your algorithm, you'll need to write a computer program in a more formal way by using a programming language like C#. You'll learn about that in the next section.

In the meantime, this section of the lesson focuses on two techniques for presenting your algorithms—namely, flowcharts and decision tables—that are more precise than a natural language but less formal and easier to use than a computer language.

### INTRODUCING FLOWCHARTS

A *flowchart* is a graphical representation of an algorithm. A flowchart is usually drawn using standard symbols. Some common flowchart symbols are shown in Table 1-1.

**Table 1-1**

Common flowchart symbols

| Flowchart Symbol | Description |
| --- | --- |
| ⬭ | Start or end of an algorithm |
| ▮ | A process or computational operation |
| ▱ | Input or output operation |
| ◆ | Decision-making operation |
| ↓ | Specifies the flow of control |

For example, Figure 1-1 shows a flowchart that inputs two numbers, compares them, and then outputs the larger number.

**Figure 1-1**

A simple flowchart that compares two numbers and outputs the larger of the two

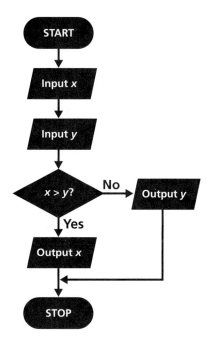

As you can see, this flowchart lists in the correct order all the necessary steps to perform the operation. The flow of control starts with the start symbol and ends at the stop symbol. The process and input/output operation symbols always have a single entry and a single exit. In contrast, the decision symbol has a single entry but multiple exits. You can test a flowchart by performing a "dry run." In a dry run, you manually trace through the steps of the flowchart with test data to check whether the correct paths are being followed.

## INTRODUCING DECISION TABLES

When an algorithm involves a large number of conditions, *decision tables* are a more compact and readable format for presenting the algorithm. Table 1-2 presents a decision table for calculating a discount. This table generates a discount percentage depending on the quantity of product purchased. The bold lines in the decision table divide the table in four quadrants. The first quadrant (top left) specifies the conditions ("Quantity < 10," etc.). The second quadrant (top right) specifies the rules. The rules are the possible combinations of the outcome of each condition. The third quadrant (bottom left) specifies the action ("Discount," in this case), and the last quadrant (bottom right) specifies the action items corresponding to each rule.

**Table 1-2**

A decision table for calculating discounts

| | | | | |
|---|---|---|---|---|
| Quantity < 10 | Y | N | N | N |
| Quantity < 50 | Y | Y | N | N |
| Quantity < 100 | Y | Y | Y | N |
| Discount | 5% | 10% | 15% | 20% |

To find out which action item to apply, you must evaluate each condition to find the matching rule and then choose the action specified in the column with the matching rule. For example, if the value of "Quantity" in the test data is 75, then the first rule evaluates to "No," the second rule evaluates to "No," and the third rule evaluates to "Yes." Therefore, you will pick the action item from the column (N, N, and Y), which sets the discount at 15%.

## Introducing C#

> C# is a popular high-level programming language that allows you to write computer programs in a human-readable format. C# is a part of the .NET Framework and benefits from the runtime support and class libraries provided by the .Framework.

As discussed in the previous section, computers need precise and complete instructions to accomplish a task. These sets of instructions are called *computer programs*, or just *programs* for short.

At the most basic level, computers use the *binary number system* to represent information and code. In this system, each value is represented using only two symbols, 0 and 1. A computer program written using the binary number system is called *binary code*.

Using binary code to program a computer is terse and extremely difficult to accomplish for any non trivial task. Thus, to simplify programming, scientists and computer engineers have built several levels of abstractions between computers and their human operators. These abstractions include software (such as operating systems, compilers, and various runtime systems) that takes responsibility for translating a human-readable program into a machine-readable program.

Most modern programs are written in a *high-level language* such as C#, Visual Basic, or Java. These languages allow you to write precise instructions in a human-readable form. A language compiler then translates the high-level language into a lower-level language that can be understood by the runtime execution system.

Each programming language provides its own set of vocabulary and grammar (also known as syntax). In this course, you'll learn how to program by using the C# programming language on the .NET Framework. The .NET Framework provides a runtime execution environment for the C# program. The Framework also contains class libraries that provide a lot of reusable core functionality that you can use directly in your C# program.

**+ MORE INFORMATION**

The .NET Framework provides three major components: a runtime execution environment, a set of class libraries that provide a great deal of reusable functionality, and language compilers for C#, Visual Basic, and Managed C++. The .NET Framework supports multiple programming languages and also has support for adding additional languages to the system. Although the syntax and vocabulary of each language may differ, each can still use the base class libraries provided by the Framework.

In this course, you will be using an integrated development environment (IDE) to develop your code. You can use either Visual Studio or the free Visual Studio Express edition to write your code. Either of these tools provides you with a highly productive environment for developing and testing your programs.

 **WRITE A C# PROGRAM**

**GET READY.** To write a C# program, perform these steps:

1. Start Visual Studio. Select **File >New Project**. Select the **Visual C# Console Application** templates.
2. Type **IntroducingCS** in the Name box. Make sure that the Create directory for solution checkbox is checked, and enter the name **Lesson01** in the Solution name box. Click **OK** to create the project.
3. When the project is created, you'll note that Visual Studio has already created a file named Program.cs and written a template for you.
4. Modify the template to resemble the following code:

```
using System;
namespace Lesson01
{
    class Program
    {
        static void Main(string[] args)
        {
            Console.WriteLine("hello, world!");
        }
    }
}
```

**TAKE NOTE***

C# is a case-sensitive programming language. As a result, typing "Class" instead of "class" (for example) will result in a syntax error.

5. Select **Debug > Start Without Debugging**, or press **Ctrl+F5**.
6. You will see the output of the program in a command Window, as shown in Figure 1-2.

**Figure 1-2**

Program output in a command window

C:\Windows\system32\cmd.exe

```
hello, world!
Press any key to continue . . .
```

 **ANOTHER WAY**

You can also execute the program by opening a command Window (cmd.exe) and then navigating to the project's output folder, which by default is the bin\debug subfolder under the project's location. Start the program by typing the name of the program in the command window and pressing Enter.

7. Press a key to close the command Window.

**PAUSE.** Leave the project open to use in the next exercise.

The program you just created is trivial in what it does, but it is nonetheless useful for understanding program structure, build, and execution. Let's first talk about the build and execution part. Here is what happens when you select the Debug > Start Without Debugging option in step 5 above:

1. Visual Studio invokes the C# compiler to translate the C# code into a lower-level language, Common Intermediate Language (CIL) code. This low-level code is stored in an executable file named (Lesson01.exe). The name of the output file can be changed by modifying a project's properties.

2. Next, Visual Studio takes the project output and requests that the operating system execute it. This is when you see the command window displaying the output.

3. When the program finishes, Visual Studio displays the following message: "Press any key to continue . . .". Note that this message is only generated when you run the program using the Start Without Debugging option.

**TAKE NOTE** *

When you select the Debug > Start Without Debugging menu option, Visual Studio automatically displays the prompt "Press any key to continue . . ." The command window then stays open for you to review the output. If, however, you select the Debug > Start Debugging option, the command window closes as soon as program execution completes. It is important to know that the Start Debugging option provides debugging capabilities such as the ability to pause a running program at a given point and review the value of various variables in memory.

If you don't use an Integrated Development Environment (IDE) like Visual Studio, you can still compile your program manually using the command-line tools. Visual Studio, of course, makes it easier and quicker to test your programs.

**TAKE NOTE** *

Before Common Intermediate Language (CIL) code can be executed, it must first be translated for the architecture of the machine on which it will run. The .NET Framework's runtime execution system takes care of this translation behind the scenes using a process called just-in-time compilation.

## UNDERSTANDING THE STRUCTURE OF A C# PROGRAM

In this section of the lesson, you'll learn about the structural elements of the simple C# program you created in the previous section.

Figure 1-3 depicts the program you created in the previous exercise with line numbers. Throughout this section, these numbers will be used to refer to different structures in the program.

**TAKE NOTE** *

To enable the display of line numbers in Visual Studio, select the Tools > Options menu. Next, expand the Text Editor node and select C#. Finally, in the Display section, check the Line Numbers option.

**Figure 1-3**

Program listing with line numbers

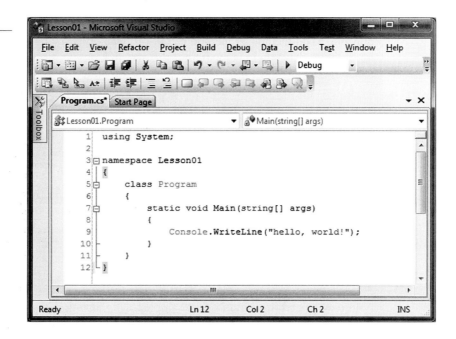

A C# program is made of one or more classes. A *class* is a set of data and methods. For example, the code in Figure 1-3 defines a single class named Program on lines 5 through 11. A class is defined by using the keyword class followed by the class name. The contents of a *class* are defined between an opening brace ({) and a closing brace (}).

You can find more information on classes in Lesson 2.

Line 3 of the code in Figure 1-3 defines a namespace, Lesson01. Namespaces are used to organize classes and uniquely identify them. The namespace and the class names are combined together to create a *fully qualified class name*. For example, the fully qualified class name for the class Program is Lesson01.Program. C# requires that the fully qualified name of a class be unique. As a result, you can't have another class by the name Program in the namespace Lesson01, but you can have a class by the name Program in another namespace, say, Lesson02. Here, the class Program defined in the namespace Lesson02 is uniquely identified by its fully qualified class name, Lesson02.Program.

You can find more information on methods in Lesson 2.

The .NET Framework provides a large number of useful classes organized into many namespaces. The System namespace contains some of the most commonly used base classes. One such class in the System namespace is Console. The Console class provides functionality for console application input and output. The line 9 of the code in Figure 1-3 refers to the Console class and calls its WriteLine method. To access the WriteLine method in an unambiguous way, you must write it like this:

System.Console.WriteLine("hello, world!");

**TAKE NOTE***

Every C# statement must end with a semicolon (;).

Because class names frequently appear in the code, writing the fully qualified class name every time will be tedious and make the program verbose. You can solve this problem by using the C# *using* directive (see the code in line 1 in Figure 1-3). The using directive allows you to use the classes in a namespace without having to fully qualify the class name.

The Program class defines a single method by the name Main (see lines 7 to 10 of the code listing in Figure 1-3). Main is a special method in that it also serves as an entry point to the program. When the runtime executes a program, it always starts at the Main method. A program can have many classes and each class can have many methods, but it should have only one Main method. A method can in turn call other methods. In line 9, the Main method is calling the WriteLine method of the System.Console class to display a string of characters on the command window—and that's how the message is displayed.

The Main method must be declared as static. A static method is callable on a class even when no instance of the class has been created. You will learn more about this in the following lesson.

## UNDERSTANDING VARIABLES

*Variables* provide temporary storage during the execution of a program.

The variables in C# are placeholders used to store values. A variable has a name and a data type. A variable's data type determines what values it can contain and what kind of operations may be performed on it. For example, the following declaration creates a variable named number of the data type int and assigns a value of 10 to the variable:

int number = 10;

When a variable is declared, a location big enough to hold the value for its data type is created in the computer memory. For example, on a 32-bit machine, a variable of data type int will need two bytes of memory. The value of a variable can be modified by another assignment, such as:

number = 20;

The above code changes the contents of the memory location identified by the name number.

A variable name must begin with a letter or an underscore and can contain only letters, numbers, or underscores. A variable name must not exceed 255 characters. A variable must also be unique within the scope in which it is defined.

## UNDERSTANDING CONSTANTS

*Constants* are data fields or local variables whose value cannot be modified.

Constants are declared by using the const keyword. For example, a constant can be declared as follows:

const int i = 10;

This declares a constant i of data type int and stores a value of 10. Once declared, the value of the constant cannot be changed.

## UNDERSTANDING DATA TYPES

*Data types* specify the type of data that you work with in a program. The data type defines the size of memory needed to store the data and the kinds of operations that can be performed on the data.

You can find more information about how to create your own data types in Lesson 2.

C# provides several built-in data types that you can use in your programs. You can also define new types by defining a data structure, such as a class or a struct. This chapter focuses on some of the most commonly used built-in data types.

Table 1-3 lists several commonly used built-in data types available in C#. The sizes listed in the table refer to a computer running a 32-bits operating system such as Windows 7, 32-bit. For a 64-bits operating system, such as Windows 7 64-bit, these sizes will be different.

**Table 1-3**

Commonly used built-in data types in C#

| DATA TYPE | SIZE | RANGE OF VALUES |
|---|---|---|
| byte | 1 byte | 0 to 255 |
| char | 2 bytes | U+0000 to U+ffff (Unicode characters) |
| short | 2 bytes | −32,768 to 32,767 |
| int | 4 bytes | −2,147,483,648 to 2,147,483,647 |
| long | 8 bytes | −9,223,372,036,854,775,808 to 9,223,372,036,854,775,807 |
| float | 4 bytes | $\pm 1.5 \times 10\text{-}45$ to $\pm 3.4 \times 1038$ |
| double | 8 bytes | $\pm 5.0e\text{-}324$ to $\pm 1.7e308$ |
| bool | 2 bytes | True or false |
| string | - | Zero or more Unicode characters |

**TAKE NOTE** *

The unsigned versions of short, int, and long are ushort, uint, and ulong, respectively. The unsigned types have the same size as their signed versions but store much larger ranges of only positive values.

All the data types listed in Table 1-3 are value types except for string, which is a reference type. The variables that are based directly on the value types contain the value. In the case of the reference type, the variable holds the address of the memory location where the actual data is stored. You will learn more about the differences between value types and reference types in Lesson 2.

## UNDERSTANDING ARRAYS

An *array* is a collection of items in which each item can be accessed by using a unique index.

An array in C# is commonly used to represent a collection of items of similar type. A sample array declaration is shown in the following code:

```
int[] numbers = { 1, 2, 3, 4, 5 };
```

This declaration creates an array identified by the name numbers. This array is capable of storing a collection of five integers. This declaration also initializes each of the array items respectively by the numbers 1 through 5.

Any array item can be directly accessed by using an index. In the .NET Framework, array indexes are zero-based. This means that to access the first element of an array, you use the index 1; to access the second element, you use the index 2, and so on.

To access an individual array element, you use the name of the array followed by the index enclosed in square brackets. For example, numbers[0] will return the value 1 from the above-declared array, and numbers[4] will return the value 5. It is illegal to access an array outside

The topic of arrays is covered in more detail in Lesson 3, Understanding General Software Development.

its defined boundaries. For example, you'll get an error if you try to access the array element numbers[5].

## UNDERSTANDING OPERATORS

> *Operators* are symbols that specify which operation to perform on the operands before returning a result.

Examples of operators include +, -, *, /, and so on, and operands can be variables, constants, literals, etc. Depending on how many operands are involved, there are three kinds of operators:

- **Unary operators:** The unary operators work with only one operand. Examples include ++x, x++, or isEven, where x is of integer data type and isEven is of Boolean data type.
- **Binary operators:** The binary operators take two operands. Examples include x + y or x > y.
- **Ternary operators:** Ternary operators take three operands. There is just one ternary operator, ?:, in C#.

Often, expressions involve more than one operator. In this case, the compiler needs to determine which operator takes precedence over the other(s). Table 1-4 lists the C# operators in order of precedence. The higher an operator is located in the table, the higher its precedence. Operators with higher precedence are evaluated before operators with lower precedence. Operators that appear in the same row have equal precedence.

**Table 1-4**

Operator precedence in C#

| CATEGORY | OPERATORS |
|---|---|
| Primary | x.y f(x) a[x] x++ x −− new typeof checked unchecked |
| Unary | + - ! ~ ++x −− x (T)x |
| Multiplicative | * / % |
| Additive | + - |
| Shift | << >> |
| Relational and type testing | < > <= >= is as |
| Equality | == != |
| Logical AND | & |
| Logical XOR | ^ |
| Logical OR | \| |
| Conditional AND | && |
| Conditional OR | \|\| |
| Conditional ternary | ?: |
| Assignment | = *= /= %= += -= <<= >>= &= ^= \|= |

The unary increment operator (++) adds 1 to the value of an identifier. Similarly, the decrement (−−) operator subtracts 1 from the value of an identifier. The unary increment and decrement can be used either as prefixes or suffixes. For example:

```
int x = 10;
x++; //value of x is now 11
++x; //value of x is now 12
```

However, the way the unary increment and decrement operators work when used as part of an assignment can affect the results. In particular, when the unary increment and decrement operators are used as prefixes, the current value of the identifier is returned prior to the increment or decrement. On the other hand, when used as a suffix, the value of the identifier is returned after the increment or decrement is complete. To understand what this means, consider the following code sample:

```
int y = x++; // the value of y is 12
int z = ++x; // the value of z is 14
```

Here, in the first statement, the value of x is returned prior to the increment. As a result, after the statement is executed, the value of y is 12 and the value of x is 13. In contrast, in the second statement, the value of x is incremented prior to returning its value for assignment. As a result, after the statement is executed, the value of both x and z is 14.

## UNDERSTANDING METHODS

> *Methods* are code blocks containing a series of statements. Methods can receive input via arguments and can return a value to the caller.

In the previous code listing, you learned about the Main method. Methods are where the action is in a program. More precisely, a method is a set of statements that are executed when the method is called.

The Main method doesn't return a value back to the calling code. This is indicated by using the void keyword. If a method were to return a value, the appropriate data type for the return value would be used instead of void.

Class members can have modifiers such as static, public, and private. These modifiers specify how and where class members can be accessed. You'll learn more about these modifiers in Lesson 2.

**CERTIFICATION READY**
Do you understand the core elements of programming, such as variables, data types, operators, and methods?
1.1

# ■ Understanding Decision Structures

**THE BOTTOM LINE**

> *Decision structures* introduce decision-making ability into a program. They enable you to branch to different sections of the code depending on the truth value of a Boolean expression.

The decision-making control structures in C# are the if, if-else, and switch statements. The following sections discuss each of these statements in more detail.

## The If Statement

> The *if statement* will execute a given sequence of statements only if the corresponding Boolean expression evaluates to true.

Sometimes in your programs, you will want a sequence of statements to be executed only if a certain condition is true. In C#, you can do this by using the if statement. Take the following steps to create a program that uses an if statement.

 **USE THE IF STATEMENT**

**GET READY.** To use the if statement, perform the following tasks:

1. Add a new Console Application project (named if_Statement) to the Lesson01 solution.
2. Add the following code to the Main method of the Program.cs class:

```
int number1 = 10;
int number2 = 20;
if (number2 > number1)
{
    Console.WriteLine("number2 is greater than number1");
}
```

3. Select **Debug > Start Without Debugging**, or press **Ctrl+F5**.
4. You will see the output of the program in a command window.
5. Press a key to close the command window.

**PAUSE.** Leave the project open to use in the next exercise.

This code is functionally equivalent to the flowchart shown in Figure 1-4.

**Figure 1-4**

The flowchart equivalent of the example if statement

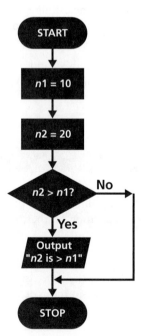

Here, the output statement will be executed only if the Boolean expression in the parentheses is true. If the expression is false, control passes to the next statement following the if statement.

In C# code, the parentheses surrounding the condition are required. However, the braces are optional if there is only one statement in the code block. So, the above if statement is equivalent to the following:

```
if (number2 > number1)
    Console.WriteLine("number2 is greater than number1");
```

In contrast, look at this example:

```
if (number2 > number1)
    Console.WriteLine("number2 is greater than number1");
Console.WriteLine(number2);
```

Here, only the first Console.WriteLine statement is part of the if statement. The second Console.WriteLine statement is always executed regardless of the value of the Boolean expression.

For clarity, it is always a good idea to enclose the statement that needs to be conditionally executed in braces.

If statements can also be nested within other if statements, as in the following example:

```
int number1 = 10;
if (number1 > 5)
{
    Console.WriteLine("number1 is greater than 5");
    if (number1 < 20)
    {
        Console.WriteLine("number1 is less than 20");
    }
}
```

Because both the conditions evaluate to true, this code would generate the following output:

```
number1 is greater than 5
number1 is less than 20
```

But what would happen if the value of number1 was 25 instead of 10 prior to the execution of the outer if statement? In this case, the first Boolean expression will evaluate to true, but the second Boolean expression will evaluate to false and the following output will be generated:

```
number1 is greater than 5
```

## The if-else Statement

The *if-else statement* allows your program to perform one action if the Boolean expression evaluates to true and a different action if the Boolean expression evaluates to false.

Take the following steps to create an example program that uses the if-else statement.

 **USE THE IF-ELSE STATEMENT**

**GET READY.** To use the if-else statement, do the following:

1. Add a new Console Application project (named ifelse_Statement) to the Lesson01 solution.

2. Add the following code to the Main method of the Program.cs class:

   TestIfElse(10);

3. Next, add the following method to the Program.cs class:

   ```
   public static void TestIfElse(int n)
   {
       if (n < 10)
       {
           Console.WriteLine("n is less than 10");
       }
       else if (n < 20)
       {
           Console.WriteLine("n is less than 20");
       }
       else if (n < 30)
       {
           Console.WriteLine("n is less than 30");
       }
       else
       {
           Console.WriteLine("n is greater than or equal to 30");
       }
   }
   ```

4. Select **Debug > Start Without Debugging**, or press **Ctrl+F5**.

5. You will see the output of the program in a command window.

6. Press a key to close the command window.

7. Modify the Main method's code to call the TestIfElse method with different values. Notice how a different branch of the if-else statement is executed as a result of your changes.

**PAUSE.** Leave the project open to use in the next exercise.

Here, the code in the TestIfElse method combines several if-else statements to test for multiple conditions. For example, if the value of n is 25, then the first two conditions ($n < 10$ and $n < 20$) will evaluate to false, but the third condition ($n < 30$) will evaluate to true. As a result, the method will print the following output:

n is less than 30

This C# program is equivalent to the flowchart shown in Figure 1-5.

**Figure 1-5**

The flowchart equivalent of the example if-else statement

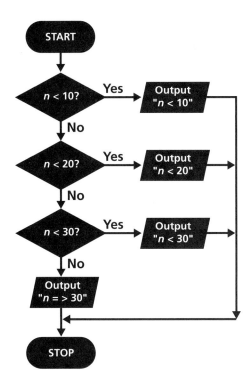

## The Switch Statement

The *switch statement* allows multi-way branching. In many cases, using a switch statement can simplify a complex combination of if-else statements.

The switch statement consists of the keyword switch, followed by an expression in parentheses, followed by a switch block. The *switch block* can include one or more *case* statements or a *default* statement. When the switch statement executes, depending on the value of the switch expression, control is transferred to a matching case statement. If the expression does not match any of the case statements, then control is transferred to the default statement. The switch expression must be surrounded by parentheses.

Take the following steps to create a program that uses the switch statement to evaluate simple expressions.

 **USE THE SWITCH STATEMENT**

**GET READY.** To use the switch statement, do the following:

1. Add a new Console Application project named switch_Statement to the Lesson01 solution.

2. Add the following code to the Main method of the Program.cs class:

   ```
   TestSwitch(10, 20, '+');
   ```

3. Add the following method to the Program.cs class:

```csharp
public static void TestSwitch(int op1, int op2, char opr)
{
    int result;
    switch (opr)
    {
        case '+':
            result = op1 + op2;
            break;
        case '−':
            result = op1 − op2;
            break;
        case '*':
            result = op1 * op2;
            break;
        case '/':
            result = op1 / op2;
            break;
        default:
            Console.WriteLine("Unknown Operator");
            return;
    }
    Console.WriteLine("Result: {0}", result);
    return;
}
```

4. Select **Debug > Start Without Debugging**, or press **Ctrl+F5**.
5. You will see the output of the program in a command window.
6. Press a key to close the command window.
7. Modify the Main method's code to call the TestSwitch method with different values. Notice how a different branch of the switch statement is executed as a result of your changes.

**PAUSE.** Leave the project open to use in the next exercise.

**TAKE NOTE***

The Console.Write and the Console.WriteLine methods can use format strings such as "Results: {0}" to format the output. Here, the string {0} stands for the first argument provided after the format string. In the TestSwitch method, the format string "{0}" is replaced by the value of the following argument, result.

Here, the TestSwitch method accepts two operands (op1 and op2) and an operator (opr) and evaluates the resulting expression. The value of the switch expression is compared to the case statements in the switch block. If there is a match, the statements following the matching case are executed. If none of the case statements match, then control is transferred to the optional default branch.

Note that there is a break statement after each case. The break statement terminates the switch statement and transfers control to the next statement outside the switch block. Using a break ensures that only one branch is executed and helps avoid programming mistakes. In fact, if you specify code after the case statement, you must include break (or another control-transfer statement, such as return) to make sure that control does not fall through from one case label to another.

However, if no code is specified after the case statement, it is okay for control to fall through to the subsequent case statement. The following code demonstrates how this might be useful:

```csharp
public static void TestSwitchFallThrough()
{
    DateTime dt = DateTime.Today;
    switch (dt.DayOfWeek)
    {
        case DayOfWeek.Monday:
        case DayOfWeek.Tuesday:
        case DayOfWeek.Wednesday:
        case DayOfWeek.Thursday:
        case DayOfWeek.Friday:
            Console.WriteLine("Today is a weekday");
            break;
        default:
            Console.WriteLine("Today is a weekend day");
            break;
    }
}
```

**CERTIFICATION READY**
Do you understand computer decision structures, such as branching and repetition?
1.2

Here, if the value of expression dt.DayofWeek is DayOfWeek.Monday, then the first case is matched, but because no code (or a control-transfer statement) is specified, the execution will fall through the next statement, resulting in display of the message "Today is a weekday" on the command window.

TAKE NOTE* You can decide whether to use if-else statements or a switch statement based on the nature of the comparison and readability of the code. For example, the code of the TestIfElse method makes decisions based on conditions that are more suited for use with if-else statements. In the TestSwitch method, the decisions are based on constant values, so the code is much more readable when written as a switch statement.

# Understanding Repetition Structures

 THE BOTTOM LINE

C# has four different control structures that allow programs to perform repetitive tasks: the while loop, the do-while loop, the for loop, and the foreach loop.

These repetition control statements can be used to execute the statements in the loop body a number of times, depending on the loop termination criterion.

A loop can also be terminated by using one of several control transfer statements that transfer control outside the loop. These statements are break, goto, return, or throw. Finally, the continue statement can be used to pass control to next iteration of the loop without exiting the loop.

## Understanding the While Loop

The *while loop* repeatedly executes a block of statements until a specified Boolean expression evaluates to false.

The general form of the while loop is as follows:

while (boolean test)

    statement

Here, a Boolean test is performed at the beginning of the loop. If the test evaluates to true, the loop body is executed and the test is performed again. If the test evaluates to false, the loop terminates and control is transferred to the next statement following the loop.

Because the Boolean test is performed before the execution of the loop, it is possible that the body of a while loop is never executed. This happens if the test evaluates to false the first time.

Take the following steps to create a program that uses the while loop.

 **USE THE WHILE LOOP**

**GET READY.** To use the while loop, perform the following tasks:

1. Add a new Console Application project named while_Statement to the Lesson01 solution.
2. Add the following code to the Main method of the Program.cs class:

   WhileTest();

3. Add the following method to the Program.cs class:

```
private static void WhileTest()
{
    int i = 1;
    while (i <= 5)
    {
        Console.WriteLine("The value of i = {0}", i);
        i++;
    }
}
```

4. Select **Debug > Start Without Debugging**, or press **Ctrl+F5**.
5. You will see the output of the program in a command window.
6. Press a key to close the command window.

**PAUSE.** Leave the project open to use in the next exercise.

In this exercise, the variable i is assigned the value 1. Next, the condition in the while loop is evaluated. Because the condition is true (1 <= 5), the code within the while statement block is executed. The value of i is written in the command window, and then the value of i is increased by 1 so that it becomes 2. Control then passes back to the while statement, and the condition is evaluated again. Because the condition is still true (2 <= 5), the statement block is executed yet again. The loop continues until the value of i becomes 6 and the condition in the while loop becomes false (6 <= 5). The above method, when executed, generates the following output:

The value of i = 1

The value of i = 2

The value of i = 3

The value of i = 4

The value of i = 5

The flowchart equivalent of this while loop is shown in Figure 1-6.

**Figure 1-6**

The flowchart equivalent of the example while loop

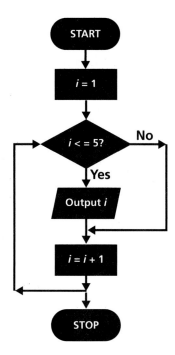

The statement in the loop, which increments the value of i, plays a critical role. If you miss this statement, the termination condition will never be achieved, and as a result, you will have a never-ending loop.

In most cases, to have a well-designed while loop, you must have three parts:

1. **Initializer:** The initializer sets the loop counter to the correct starting value. In the above example, the variable i is set to 1 before the loop begins.

2. **Loop test:** The loop test specifies the termination condition for the loop. In the above example, the expression (i <= 5) is the condition expression.

3. **Termination expression:** The termination expression changes the value of the loop counter in such a way that the termination condition in achieved. In the above example, the expression i+ + is the termination expression.

> TAKE NOTE
>
> To avoid an infinite loop, you must make sure that your while loop is designed in such a way that it leads to termination.

## Understanding the Do-While Loop

> The *do-while loop* repeatedly executes a block of statements until a specified Boolean expression evaluates to false. The do-while loop tests the condition at the bottom of the loop.

The do-while loop is similar to the while loop but, unlike the while loop, the body of the do-while loop must be executed at least once.

The general form of the do-while loop is as follows:

```
do
    statement
while (boolean test);
```

Take the following steps to create a program that uses the do-while loop.

> TAKE NOTE
>
> With the do-while loop, the Boolean test must be placed inside parentheses. If more than one statement needs to be executed as part of a do-while loop, these statements must be placed together inside curly braces.

**USE THE DO-WHILE LOOP**

**GET READY.** To use the do-while loop, do the following tasks:

1. Add a new Console Application project named dowhile_Statement to the Lesson01 solution.

2. Add the following code to the Main method of the Program.cs class:

   DoWhileTest();

3. Add the following method to the Program.cs class:

```
private static void DoWhileTest()
{
    int i = 1;
    do
    {
        Console.WriteLine("The value of i = {0}", i);
        i++;
    }
    while (i <= 5);
}
```

4. Select **Debug > Start Without Debugging**, or press **Ctrl+F5**.

5. You'll see the output of the program in a command window.

6. Press a key to close the command window.

**PAUSE.** Leave the project open to use in the next exercise.

In this exercise, after the variable i is assigned the value 1, the control directly enters the loop. At this point, the code within the do-while statement block is executed. Specifically, the value of i is written in the command window and the value of i is increased by 1 so that it becomes 2. Next, the condition for the do-while loop is evaluated. Because the condition is still true (2 <= 5), control passes back to the do-while statement, and the statement block is executed **again.** The loop continues until the value of i becomes 6 and the condition of the do-while loop becomes false (6 <= 5). The above method, when executed, generates the same output as the WhileTest method.

The choice between a while loop and a do-while loop depends on whether you want the loop to execute at least once. If you want the loop to execute zero or more times, choose the while loop. In contrast, if you want the loop to execute one or more times, choose the do-while loop.

## Understanding the For Loop

TAKE NOTE*

With the for loop, the three control expressions must be placed inside parentheses. If more than one statement needs to be executed as part of the loop, these statements must be placed together inside curly braces.

The *for loop* combines the three elements of iteration—the initialization expression, the termination condition expression, and the counting expression—into a more readable code.

The for loop is similar to the while loop; it allows a statement or a statement block to be executed repeatedly until an expression evaluates to false. The general form of the for loop is as follows:

for (init-expr; cond-expr; count-expr)

   statement

As you can see, the for loop combines the three essential control expressions of an iteration. This results in more readable code. The for loop is especially useful for creating iterations that must execute a specified number of times.

Take the following steps to create a program that uses the for loop.

 **USE THE FOR LOOP**

**GET READY.** To use the for loop, perform the following tasks:

1. Add a new Console Application project named for_Statement to the Lesson01 solution.
2. Add the following code to the Main method of the Program.cs class:
   ForTest();
3. Add the following method to the Program.cs class:

```
private static void ForTest()
{
    for(int i = 1; i<= 5; i++)
    {
        Console.WriteLine("The value of i = {0}", i);
    }
}
```

4. Select **Debug > Start Without Debugging**, or press **Ctrl+F5**.
5. You will see the output of the program in a command window.
6. Press a key to close the command window.

**PAUSE.** Leave the project open to use in the next exercise.

The ForTest method, when executed, generates the same output as the WhileTest method. Here, the variable i is created within the scope of the for loop and its value is assigned to 1. The loop continues as long as the value of i is less than or equal to 5. After the loop body, the count-expr is evaluated and the control goes back to the cond-expr.

All the control expressions of a for loop are optional. For example, you can omit all the expressions to create an infinite loop like this:

```
for (; ;)
{
    //do nothing
}
```

## Understanding the Foreach Loop

The *foreach loop* is useful for iterating through the elements of a collection.

The foreach loop can be thought of as enhanced version of the for loop for iterating through collections such as arrays and lists. The general form of the foreach statement is as follows:

```
foreach (ElementType element in collection)
    statement
```

The control expressions for the foreach loop must be placed inside parentheses. If more than one statement needs to be executed as part of the loop, these statements must be placed together inside curly braces.

Take the following steps to create a program that shows how the foreach loop provides a simple way to iterate through a collection.

 **USE THE FOREACH LOOP**

**GET READY.** To use the foreach loop, do the following:

1. Add a new Console Application project named foreach_Statement to the Lesson01 solution.
2. Add the following code to the Main method of the Program.cs class:
   ForEachTest();
3. Add the following method to the Program.cs class:

```
private static void ForEachTest()
{
    int[] numbers = { 1, 2, 3, 4, 5 };
    foreach (int i in numbers)
    {
        Console.WriteLine("The value of i = {0}", i);
    }
}
```

4. Select **Debug > Start Without Debugging**, or press **Ctrl+F5**.
5. You will see the output of the program in a command window.
6. Press a key to close the command window.

**PAUSE.** Leave the project open to use in the next exercise.

In this exercise, the loop sequentially iterates through every element of the collection, numbers it, and displays it in the command window. This method generates the same output as the ForTest method.

## Understanding Recursion

*Recursion* is a programming technique that causes a method to call itself in order to compute a result.

Recursion and iteration are related. You can write a method that generates the same results with either recursion or iteration. Usually, the nature of the problem itself will help you choose between an iterative or a recursive solution. For example, a recursive solution is more elegant when you can define the solution of a problem in terms of a smaller version of the same problem.

To better understand this concept, take the example of the factorial operation from mathematics. The general recursive definition for n factorial (written n!) is as follows:

$$n! = \begin{cases} 1 & \text{if } n = 0, \\ (n - 1)! \times n & \text{if } n > 0. \end{cases}$$

According to this definition, if the number is 0, the factorial is one. If the number is larger than zero, the factorial is the number multiplied by the factorial of the next smaller number.

For example, you can break down 3! like this: $3! = 3 * 2! \rightarrow 3 * 2 * 1! \rightarrow 3 * 2 * 1 * 0! \rightarrow 3 * 2 * 1 * 1 \rightarrow 6$.

Take the following steps to create a program that presents a recursive solution to a factorial problem.

 **USE THE RECURSIVE METHOD**

**GET READY.** To use the recursive method, perform the following actions:

1. Add a new Console Application project named RecursiveFactorial to the Lesson01 solution.
2. Add the following code to the Main method of the Program.cs class:

   Factorial(5);

3. Add the following method to the Program.cs class:

   ```
   public static int Factorial(int n)
   {
       if (n == 0)
       {
           return 1; //base case
       }
       else
       {
           return n * Factorial(n - 1); //recursive case
       }
   }
   ```

4. Select **Debug > Start Without Debugging**, or press **Ctrl+F5**.
5. You will see the output of the program in a command window.
6. Press a key to close the command window.
7. Modify the Main method to pass a different value to the Factorial method, and note the results.

**PAUSE.** Leave the project open to use in the next exercise.

As seen in the above exercise, a recursive solution has two distinct parts:

- **Base case:** This is the part that specifies the terminating condition and doesn't call the method again. The base case in the Factorial method is n == 0. If you don't have a base case in your recursive algorithm, you create an infinite recursion. An infinite recursion will cause your computer to run out of memory and throw a System. StackOverflowException exception.

**CERTIFICATION READY**
Can you identify the appropriate methods for handling repetition?
1.3

- **Recursive case:** This is the part that moves the algorithm toward the base case. The recursive case in the Factorial method is the else part, where you call the method again but with a smaller value progressing toward the base case.

# ■ Understanding Exception Handling

 **THE BOTTOM LINE** The .NET Framework supports standard exception handling to raise and handle runtime errors. In this section, you'll learn how to use the try, catch, and finally keywords to handle exceptions.

An *exception* is an error condition that occurs during the execution of a C# program. When this happens, the runtime creates an object to represent the error and "throws" it. Unless you "catch" the exception by writing proper exception-handling code, program execution will terminate.

For example, if you attempt to divide an integer by zero, a DivideByZeroException exception will be thrown. In the .NET Framework, an exception is represented by using an object of the System.Exception class or one of its derived classes. There are predefined exception classes that represent many commonly occurring error situations, such as the DivideByZeroException mentioned earlier. If you are designing an application that needs to throw any application-specific exceptions, you should create a custom exception class that derives from the System.Exception class.

## Handling Exceptions

To handle exceptions, place the code that throws the exceptions inside a try block and place the code that handles the exceptions inside a catch block.

The following exercise shows how to use a try-catch block to handle an exception. The exercise uses the File.OpenText method to open a disk file. This statement will execute just fine in the normal case, but if the file (or permission to read the file) is missing, then an exception will be thrown.

 **HANDLE EXCEPTIONS**

**GET READY.** To handle exceptions, perform the following steps:

1. Add a new Console Application project named HandlingExceptions to the Lesson01 solution.
2. Add the following code to the Main method of the Program.cs class:
   ExceptionTest();
3. Add the following method to the Program.cs class:

```
private static void ExceptionTest()
{
    StreamReader sr = null;
    try
    {
        sr = File.OpenText(@"c:\data.txt");
        Console.WriteLine(sr.ReadToEnd());
    }
    catch (FileNotFoundException fnfe)
    {
        Console.WriteLine(fnfe.Message);
    }
    catch(Exception ex)
    {
        Console.WriteLine(ex.Message);
    }
}
```

TAKE NOTE*

The StreamReader class is part of the System.IO namespace. When running this code, you'll need to add a using directive for the System.IO namespace.

4. Create a text file ("data.txt") using Notepad or Visual Studio on the C: drive. It is acceptable to create the file at a different location, but if you do so, remember to modify the file location in the program. Enter some text in the file.

5. Select **Debug > Start Without Debugging**, or press **Ctrl+F5**.

6. You will see the contents of the text file displayed in a command window.

7. Press a key to close the command window.

8. Delete the data.txt file and run the program again. This time, you'll get a FileNotFoundException exception, and an appropriate message will be displayed in the output window.

**PAUSE.** Leave the project open to use in the next exercise.

TAKE NOTE*

In the ExceptionTest method, it is incorrect to change the order of the two catch blocks. The more specific exceptions need to be listed before the generic exceptions, or else you'll get compilation errors.

To handle an exception, you enclose the statements that could cause the exception in a try block, then you add catch blocks to handle one or more exceptions. In this example, in addition to handling the more specific FileNotFoundException exception, we are also using a catch block with more generic exceptions to catch all other exceptions. The exception name for a catch block must be enclosed within parentheses. The statements that are executed when an exception is caught must be enclosed within curly braces.

TAKE NOTE*

A try block must have at least a catch block or a finally block associated with it.

Code execution stops when an exception occurs. The runtime searches for a catch statement that matches the type of exception. If the first catch block doesn't catch the raised exception, control moves to the next catch block, and so on. If the exception is not handled in the method, the runtime checks for the catch statement in the calling code and continues for the rest of the call stack.

## Using Try-Catch-Finally

The *finally block* is used in association with the try block. The finally block is always executed regardless of whether an exception is thrown. The finally block is often used to write clean-up code.

When an exception occurs, it often means that some lines of code after the exception were not executed. This may leave your program in a dirty or unstable state. To prevent such situations, you can use the finally statement to guarantee that certain cleanup code is always executed. This may involve closing connections, releasing resources, or setting variables to their expected values. Let's look at a finally block in the following exercise.

 **USE TRY-CATCH-FINALLY**

**GET READY.** To use the try-catch-finally statement, perform the following steps:

1. Add a new Console Application project named trycatchfinally to the Lesson01 solution.

2. Add the following code to the Main method of the Program.cs class:

```
TryCatchFinallyTest();
```

**3.** Add the following method to the Program.cs class:

```
private static void TryCatchFinallyTest()
{
    StreamReader sr = null;
    try
    {
        sr = File.OpenText("data.txt");
        Console.WriteLine(sr.ReadToEnd());
    }
    catch (FileNotFoundException fnfe)
    {
        Console.WriteLine(fnfe.Message);
    }
    catch (Exception ex)
    {
        Console.WriteLine(ex.Message);
    }
    finally
    {
        if (sr != null)
        {
            sr.Close();
        }
    }
}
```

**4.** Create a text file ("data.txt") using Notepad or Visual Studio on the C: drive. It is acceptable to create the file at a different location, but if you do so, remember to modify the file location in the program. Enter some text in the file.

**5.** Select **Debug > Start Without Debugging**, or press **Ctrl+F5**.

**6.** You will see the contents of the text file displayed in a command window.

**7.** Press a key to close the command window.

**8.** Delete the data.txt file and run the program again. This time, you'll get a FileNotFoundException exception, and an appropriate message will be displayed in the output window.

**CERTIFICATION READY**
Do you understand how to handle errors in your programs?
1.4

In this exercise, the program makes sure that the StreamReader object is closed and any resources are released when the operation completes. The code in the finally block is executed regardless of whether an exception is thrown.

## SKILL SUMMARY

**IN THIS LESSON, YOU LEARNED THE FOLLOWING:**

- An algorithm is a set of ordered and finite steps to solve a given problem. You may find it useful to express an algorithm as a flowchart or a decision table before you develop a formal computer program.
- The C# programming language is a part of the .NET Framework and benefits from the runtime support and class libraries provided by the .NET Framework.
- Main is a special method because it also serves as an entry point to a program. When the runtime executes a program, it always starts at the Main method.
- Variables in C# are placeholders used to store values. A variable has a name and a data type. A variable's data type determines what value it can contain and what kind of operations may be performed on it.

- Operators are symbols, such as +, -, *, and /, that specify which operation to perform on one or more operands before returning a result.
- If-else statements allow a program to perform one action if the Boolean expression evaluates to true and a different action if the Boolean expression evaluates to false.
- The switch statement allows multi-way branching. In many cases, using a switch statement can simplify a complex combination of if-else statements.
- C# has four different control structures that allow programs to perform repetitive tasks: the while loop, the do-while loop, the for loop, and the foreach loop.
- The while and do-while loops repeatedly execute a block of statements until a specified Boolean expression evaluates to false. The do-while loop tests the condition at the bottom of the loop.
- The for loop combines the three elements of iteration—the initialization statement, the termination condition, and the increment/decrement statement—into more readable code.
- The foreach loop is useful for iterating through the elements of a collection.
- Recursion is a programming technique that causes a method to call itself in order to compute a result.
- The .NET Framework supports standard exception handling to raise and handle runtime errors. To handle exceptions, place the code that throws exceptions inside a try block, and place the code that handles the exceptions inside a catch block.
- The finally block is used in association with the try block. The finally block is always executed regardless of whether an exception is thrown. The finally block is often used to write clean-up code.

# ■ Knowledge Assessment

## Fill in the Blank

*Complete the following sentences by writing the correct word or words in the blanks provided.*

1. The _____ statement selects for execution a statement list having an associated label that corresponds to the value of an expression.
2. The _____ loop tests the condition at the bottom of the loop instead of at the top.
3. The only operator that takes three arguments is the _____ operator.
4. The _____ loop is the most compact way to iterate through the items in a collection.
5. On a 32-bit computer, a variable of int data type takes _____ bytes of memory.
6. To access the first element of an array, you use an index of _____.
7. _____ is a programming technique that causes a method to call itself in order to compute a result.
8. _____ are data fields or local variables whose value cannot be modified.
9. When an algorithm involves a large number of conditions, a(n) _____ is a compact and readable format for presenting the algorithm.
10. A(n) _____ is a graphical representation of an algorithm.

## Multiple Choice

*Circle the letter that corresponds to the best answer.*

1.  Write the following code snippet:

    ```
    int n = 20;
    int d = n++ + 5;
    ```

    What will be the value of d after this code snippet is executed?
    a. 25
    b. 26
    c. 27
    d. 28

2.  Write the following code snippet:

    ```
    private static void WhileTest()
    {
        int i = 1;
        while (i < 5)
        {
            Console.WriteLine("The value of i = {0}", i);
            i++;
        }
    }
    ```

    How many times will the while loop be executed in this code snippet?
    a. 0
    b. 1
    c. 4
    d. 5

3.  Write the following code snippet:

    ```
    int number1 = 10;
    int number2 = 20;
    if (number2 > number1)
    Console.WriteLine("number1");
    Console.WriteLine("number2");
    ```

    What output will be displayed after this code snippet is executed?
    a. number1
    b. number2
    c. number1
       number2
    d. number2
       number1

4.  In a switch statement, if none of the case statements match the switch expression, then control is transferred to which statement?
    a. break
    b. continue
    c. default
    d. return

5.  You need to write code that closes a connection to a database, and you need to make sure this code is always executed regardless of whether an exception is thrown. Where should you write this code?
    a. Within a try block
    b. Within a catch block

    **c.** Within a finally block

    **d.** Within the Main method

6. You need to store values ranging from 0 to 255. You also need to make sure that your program minimizes memory use. Which data type should you use to store these values?

    **a.** byte

    **b.** char

    **c.** short

    **d.** int

7. If you don't have a base case in your recursive algorithm, you create an infinite recursion. An infinite recursion will cause your program to throw an exception. Which exception will your program throw in such a case?

    **a.** OutOfMemoryException

    **b.** StackOverflowException

    **c.** DivideByZeroException

    **d.** InvalidOperationException

8. You are learning how to develop repetitive algorithms in C#. You write the following method:

```
private static void ForTest()
{
    for(int i = 1; i < 5;)
    {
        Console.WriteLine("The value of i = {0}", i);
    }
}
```

    How many repetitions will the for loop in this code perform?

    **a.** 0

    **b.** 4

    **c.** 5

    **d.** Infinite repetitions

9. Which of the following C# features should you use to organize code and create globally unique types?

    **a.** Assembly

    **b.** Namespace

    **c.** Class

    **d.** Data type

10. You write the following code snippet:

```
int[] numbers = {1, 2, 3, 4};
int val = numbers[1];
```

    You also create a variable of the RectangleHandler type like this:

```
RectangleHandler handler;
```

    What is the value of the variable val after this code snippet is executed?

    **a.** 1

    **b.** 2

    **c.** 3

    **d.** 4

# ■ Competency Assessment

## Scenario 1-1: Converting a Decision Table into a C# Program

You are developing an invoicing application that calculates discount percentages based on the quantity of a product purchased. The logic for calculating discounts is listed in the following decision table. If you need to write a C# method that uses the same logic to calculate the discount, how would you write such a program?

| | | | | |
|---|---|---|---|---|
| Quantity < 10 | Y | N | N | N |
| Quantity < 50 | Y | Y | N | N |
| Quantity < 100 | Y | Y | Y | N |
| Discount | 5% | 10% | 15% | 20% |

## Scenario 1-2: Converting a Flowchart into a C# Program

You are developing a library of mathematical functions. You first develop the following flow-chart describing the algorithm for calculating the factorial of a number. You need to write an equivalent C# program for this flowchart. How would you write such a program?

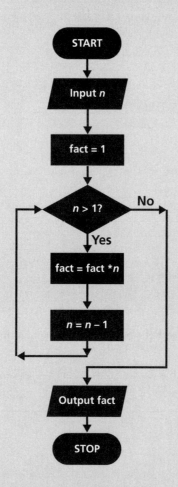

# ■ Proficiency Assessment

### Scenario 1-3: Handling Exceptions

You are writing code for a simple arithmetic library. You decide to create a method named Divide that takes two arguments, x and y, and returns the value of x/y. You need to catch any arithmetic exceptions that might be thrown for errors in arithmetic, casting, or data type conversions. You also need to catch any other exceptions that may be thrown from the code. To address this requirement, you need to create properly structured exception-handling code. How would you write such a program?

### Scenario 1-4: Creating a Recursive Algorithm

You are developing a library of utility functions for your application. You need to write a method that takes an integer and counts the number of significant digits in it. You need to create a recursive program to solve this problem. How would you write such a program?

# Introduction to Object-Oriented Programming

## LESSON SKILL MATRIX

| Skills/Concepts | MTA Exam Objective | MTA Exam Objective Number |
| --- | --- | --- |
| Understanding Objects | Understand the fundamentals of classes. | 2.1 |
| Understanding Values and References | Understand computer storage and data types. | 1.1 |
| Understanding Encapsulation | Understand encapsulation. | 2.4 |
| Understanding Inheritance | Understand inheritance. | 2.2 |
| Understanding Polymorphism | Understand polymorphism. | 2.3 |
| Understanding Interfaces | Understand encapsulation. | 2.4 |

## KEY TERMS

| | | |
| --- | --- | --- |
| access modifier | encapsulation | polymorphism |
| accessors | events | properties |
| abstract classes | inheritance | reference type |
| auto implemented properties | interfaces | sealed classes |
| class | method | signature |
| constructors | namespace | static numbers |
| delegates | objects | value type |

You are a software developer for the Northwind Corporation. You work as part of a team to develop computer programs that solve complex business problems. Any programs that you write must be easy to understand and maintain over a long period of time. Therefore, you need to develop programs using techniques that encourage code reuse, extensibility, and collaboration. Also, rather than thinking about your programs primarily as lists of methods, you opt to model them on real-world business concepts, such as customers, products, suppliers, and the interactions among them.

## Understanding Objects

**THE BOTTOM LINE**

Object-oriented programming is a programming technique that makes use of objects. *Objects* are self-contained data structures that consist of properties, methods, and events. Properties specify the data represented by an object, methods specify an object's behavior, and events provide communication between objects.

### Thinking in an Object-Oriented Way

A software object is conceptually similar to a real-world object.

A great way to start thinking in an object-oriented way is to look at real-world objects, such as cars, phones, music players, etc. You'll notice that these objects all have state and behavior. For example, cars have not only various states (e.g., model name, color, current speed, fuel level), but also various behaviors (e.g., accelerate, brake, change gear). Similarly, you'll notice that some objects are simple, whereas others are complex. Most complex objects (such as a car) are made up of smaller objects that in turn have their own state and behavior. You'll also notice that although a car is a complex object, you only need to know a few things in order to interact with it. As you drive a car, for example, you simply invoke a behavior such as accelerate or brake; you are spared from knowing the many thousands of internal details at work under the hood.

A software object is conceptually similar to a real-world object. Within the software environment, an object stores its state in fields and exposes its behavior through methods. When a method is invoked on an object, you get a well-defined functionality without the need to worry about the inner complexity of the object or the method itself. This concept of hiding complexity is called *encapsulation*, and it is one of many features of objected-oriented programming that you'll learn more about in this lesson.

### Understanding Classes

A *class* is the template from which individual objects are created.

In the real world, objects need a template that defines how they should be built. All objects created from the same template look and behave in a similar way. For example, think about a particular make and model of car.

In the software world, a class is the template from which individual objects are created. An object is also known as an *instance* of a class.

### CREATE A CLASS

**GET READY.** Before you begin these steps, be sure to launch Microsoft Visual Studio and open a new Console Application Project named Lesson02. Then, perform the following tasks:

1. Add a new Visual C# class named Rectangle to the project.
2. Replace the code for the Rectangle class with the following code:

```csharp
class Rectangle
{
    private double length;
```

```
            private double width;
            public Rectangle(double l, double w)
            {
                length = l;
                width = w;
            }
            public double GetArea()
            {
                return length * width;
            }
    }
```

3. Select **Build** > **Lesson02** to build the project. Ensure that there are no errors.

**PAUSE.** Leave the project open to use in the next exercise.

You have just created a new C# class named Rectangle. A new class is defined by using the keyword *class*. Here, the Rectangle class has two data fields, length and width. These fields are defined by using the *access modifier* private. An access modifier specifies what region of the code will have access to a field. For example, the access modifier public will not limit access, but the access modifier private will limit access within the class in which the field is defined.

This class also defines a method named GetArea. But what, exactly, is a method?

## UNDERSTANDING METHODS

A *method* is a block of code containing a series of statements.

In the software world, a method defines the actions or operations supported by a class. A method is defined by specifying the access level, the return type, the name of the method, and an optional list of parameters in parentheses followed by a block of code enclosed in braces. For instance, in the previous example, the class Rectangle defines a single method named GetArea. For GetArea, the access level is public, the return type is double, the method name is GetArea, the parameter list is empty, and the block of code is a single return statement.

A method can return a value to the calling code. If a method does not intend to return any value, its return type is specified by the keyword *void*. The method must use a *return* statement to return a value. The return statement terminates the execution of the method and returns the specified value to the calling code. The data type of the value returned from a method must match the return type specified on the method's declaration line.

To return to the earlier example, the return type of the method GetArea is double, which means that the GetArea method must return a value of the type double. The GetArea method satisfies this requirement by returning the expression length * width, which is a double value.

The following code defines an InitFields method that takes two parameters of type double and returns void:

```
public void InitFields(double l, double w)
{
    length = l;
    width = w;
}
```

The InitFields method takes two parameters and uses the parameter values to respectively assign the data field length and width. When a method's return type is void, a return statement with no value can be used. If a return statement is not used, as in the InitFields method, the method will stop executing when it reaches the end of the code block. The InitFields method can be used to properly initialize the value of the data fields, but as you'll learn in the following section, constructors already give you a way of initializing a class.

## UNDERSTANDING CONSTRUCTORS

*Constructors* are used to initialize the data members of the object.

Constructors are special class methods that are executed when a new instance of a class is created. Constructors are used to initialize the data members of the object. Constructors must have exactly the same name as the class, and they do not have a return type. Multiple constructors, each with a unique signature, can be defined for a class.

A constructor that takes no arguments is called the *default constructor*. If a class is defined without any constructor, an invisible default constructor that does absolutely nothing is automatically generated.

It is often useful to have additional constructors to provide more ways through which an object is initialized. The Rectangle class, defined earlier, is only one way to create and initialize its object: by calling the constructor that accepts two parameters, both of the default data type.

## CREATING OBJECTS

*Objects* are created from the templates defined by classes.

 **CREATE AN OBJECT**

**GET READY.** For this activity, use the console application project (Lesson 02) that you created in the previous exercise. Then, perform these steps:

1. Modify the code of the Program class to the following:

```
class Program
{
    static void Main(string[] args)
    {
        Rectangle rect = new Rectangle(10.0, 20.0);
        double area = rect.GetArea();
        Console.WriteLine("Area of Rectangle: {0}",
            area);
    }
}
```

2. Select **Debug > Start Without Debugging**. A console window will pop up to display the area of the rectangle.

3. SAVE your project.

**PAUSE.** Leave the project open to use in the next exercise.

The class Rectangle provides only one way to construct an instance of the class: by calling a constructor with two arguments of the double data type. Here, you create an object by using the *new* keyword followed by the call to the appropriate class constructor.

When the code executes, an object of Rectangle type is created in the heap memory. A reference to this memory is stored inside the variable rect, and the variable rect is stored on the stack. Later in this block of code, you can use rect to refer to and manipulate the object that was just created.

Using the object's reference, you can access the class members. For example, the code calls the method GetArea on the object, and the value returned by the method is stored in the variable area. The data fields, length and width, of the object rect are not accessible here because they are marked as private in the class definition.

## UNDERSTANDING PROPERTIES

*Properties* allow you to access class data in a safe and flexible way.

Properties are class members that can be accessed like data fields but contain code like a method. Properties are often used to expose the data fields of a class in a more controlled manner. For example, a private field can be exposed by using a public property, but it is not necessary to use properties in this way.

A property has two *accessors*, get and set. The get accessor is used to return the property value, and the set accessor is used to assign a new value to the property. A property is often defined as public and, by convention, always has a name that begins with a capital letter. In contrast, the convention for naming private data fields is to begin with a lower-case letter.

 **CREATE PROPERTIES**

**USE** the project you saved in the previous exercise. Then, complete the following tasks:

1. Modify the code of class Rectangle as shown below. In this code, the constructor is removed and two properties are inserted:

```
class Rectangle
{
    private double length;
    private double width;
    public double Length
    {
        get
        {
            return length;
        }
        set
        {
            if ( value > 0.0)
                length = value;
        }
    }
    public double Width
    {
        get
        {
            return width;
        }
```

```
            set
            {
                if (value > 0.0 )
                    width = value;
            }
        }
        public double GetArea()
        {
            return length * width;
        }
    }
```

2. Next, modify the code of the Program class to the following:

```
class Program
{
 static void Main(string[] args)
 {
        Rectangle rect = new Rectangle();
        rect.Length = 10.0;
        rect.Width = 20.0;
        double area = rect.GetArea();
        Console.WriteLine(
            "Area of Rectangle: {0}", area);
    }
}
```

3. Select **Debug > Start Without Debugging**. A console window will pop up to display the area of the rectangle.

4. SAVE your project.

**PAUSE.** Leave the project open to use in the next exercise.

In this exercise, you have modified the class Rectangle to introduce two properties, Length and Width. Properties are often defined with a public access modifier. In the code for the property Length, the get accessor simply returns the value of the data field length. However, the set accessor checks for the value being assigned (using the *value* keyword) to the property and modifies the data field length only if the value is positive. The private fields length and width are also called backing fields for the properties that respectively expose them.

The class Rectangle also does not declare any explicit constructor. In this case, the users of the class (the Main method) need to use the default constructor and rely on properties to initialize the class data.

The Main method uses the properties Length and Width to set the data for the rect object. Trying to set either Length or Width to a negative value will be ignored, and in this case, the data fields will still have their original value of 0.

When defining properties, you can exclude either the get or the set accessor. If you don't include a set accessor, you don't provide a way to set the value of the property, and as a result, you have a read-only property. On the other hand, if you don't include the get accessor, you don't provide a way to get the value of the property, and as a result, you have a write-only property.

## UNDERSTANDING AUTO-IMPLEMENTED PROPERTIES

*Auto-implemented properties* simplify property declarations.

C# introduced auto-implemented properties beginning with version 3 to simplify property declaration when there is no additional logic specified in the get and set accessors. For example, without the validation checks, the Length and Width properties are defined like this:

```
private double length;
private double width;

public double Length
{
    get
    {
        return length;
    }
    set
    {
        length = value;
    }
}
public double Width
{
    get
    {
        return width;
    }
    set
    {
        width = value;
    }
}
```

In comparison, with C# auto-implemented properties, the simplified syntax for property declaration becomes:

```
public double Length { get; set; }
public double Width { get; set; }
```

In this case, the backing fields for the properties are defined behind the scenes and are not directly accessible by the code.

The auto-implemented properties used with default constructors can also simplify the creation and initialization of objects. For example, now an object can be created and initialized as follows:

```
static void Main(string[] args)
{
    Rectangle rect = new Rectangle
        { Length = 10.0, Width = 20.0 };
    Console.WriteLine(
        "Area of Rectangle: {0}", rect.GetArea());
}
```

## USING THE *THIS* KEYWORD

The *this* keyword can be used to access members from within constructors, instance methods, and accessors of instance properties.

The *this* keyword is a reference to the current instance of the class. You can use the *this* keyword to refer to any member of the current object. For example, earlier in this chapter, the Rectangle class was written as follows:

```
class Rectangle
{
    private double length;
    private double width;
    public Rectangle(double l, double w)
    {
        length = l;
        width = w;
    }
    public double GetArea()
    {
        return length * width;
    }
}
```

However, it could have been written like this:

```
class Rectangle
{
    private double length;
    private double width;
    public Rectangle(double l, double w)
    {
        this.length = l;
        this.width = w;
    }
    public double GetArea()
    {
        return this.length * this.width;
    }
}
```

As you can see, in the second example, the *this* keyword was used within the constructor and the GetArea method to refer to the data fields of the current object of the Rectangle class. Although it was not necessary to use the *this* keyword in this case, using it provides more flexibility in naming the method parameters. For example, you could define the constructor as follows:

```
public Rectangle(double length, double width)
{
    // the parameter names length and width
    // shadow the class members length and
    // width in this scope
    this.length = length;
    this.width = width;
}
```

**TAKE NOTE** ★

In C#, the characters // are used to add single-line comments to the code. The text following the // characters is ignored by the compiler. Multi-line comments start with the characters /* and end with the characters */.

Within the scope of the definition of the Rectangle constructor, the names length and width will now refer to the parameter being passed. The names of the data fields have been shadowed and can be only accessed by using the *this* keyword.

## UNDERSTANDING DELEGATES

> *Delegates* are special types that are used to encapsulate a method with a specific signature.

Delegates are special objects that can hold a reference to a method with a specific signature. A delegate is defined by using the delegate keyword. For instance, you can define a delegate as follows:

```
public delegate void RectangleHandler(Rectangle rect);
```

The delegate definition specifies the signature of the method whose reference can be held by a delegate object. For example, in the above code, you define a RectangleHandler delegate that can hold references to a method that returns void and accepts a single parameter of the Rectangle type.

So, if you have a method with a similar signature, it is an ideal candidate for assignment to a delegate instance. For example:

```
public void DisplayArea(Rectangle rect)
{
    Console.WriteLine(rect.GetArea());
}
```

The delegate type can be used to declare a variable that can refer to any method with the same signature as the delegate. For example, you can say:

```
RectangleHandler handler;
```

And you can then assign the method to the delegate using the following syntax:

```
handler += new RectangleHandler(DisplayArea);
```

Alternatively, you can use the shortcut syntax shown below:

```
handler += DisplayArea;
```

Notice that the syntax uses the addition operation. This means that you can associate more than one method (of compatible signature), thereby creating an invocation list of one or more methods.

Finally, a call to a delegate can be made by a method-calling syntax, like this:

```
Rectangle rect = new Rectangle (10, 20);
handler(rect);
```

When the delegate is called in this way, it invokes all the methods in its invocation list. In this specific example, the handler object refers to only one method DisplayArea, and therefore, the DisplayArea method will be invoked with the rect object as a parameter.

Among many other applications, delegates form the basis for event declarations, as discussed in the next section.

## UNDERSTANDING EVENTS

> *Events* are a way for a class to notify other classes or objects when something of interest happens. The class that sends the notification is called a publisher of the event. The class that receives the notification is called the subscriber of the event.

Events are easy to understand in the context of a graphical user interface (GUI). For example, when a user clicks on a button, a Click event occurs. Multiple user interface elements can subscribe to this event and change their visual state accordingly (for example, some controls are enabled or disabled). In this type of event communication, the event publishers do not need to know which objects subscribe to the events that are being raised.

Events are not just limited to GUI programming. In fact, events play an important role in .NET Framework class libraries as a way for objects to signal any change in their state. You'll work with events in practically all programs.

When you define events, you generally need two pieces of information:

- A delegate that connects the event with its handler method(s)
- A class that contains the event data. This class is usually derived from the EventArgs class

To define an event, you can use a custom delegate. However, in most cases, if your event holds no event-specific data, using the predefined delegate EventHandler is sufficient. The EventHandler delegate is defined as follows:

public delegate void EventHandler(Object sender, EventArgs e);

Here, the sender parameter is a reference to the object that raises the event, and the e parameter is a reference to an event data object that contains no event data.

The EventArgs class is used by events that do not pass any event-related information to an event handler when an event is raised. If the event handler requires event-related information, the application must derive a class from the EventArgs class to hold the event-related data.

 **PUBLISH AND SUBSCRIBE TO EVENTS**

**USE** the project you saved in the previous exercise to carry out the following tasks:

1. Modify the code of class Rectangle as shown below:

```
class Rectangle
{
    public event EventHandler Changed;
    private double length;
    public double Length
    {
        get
        {
            return length;
        }
        set
        {
            length = value;
            Changed(this, EventArgs.Empty);
        }
    }
}
```

2. Modify the code of the Program class to the following:

```
class Program
{
    static void Main(string[] args)
    {
        Rectangle r = new Rectangle();
```

---

**TAKE NOTE ***

The EventArgs.Empty field represents an event with no event data. This field is equivalent to having a read-only instance of the EventArgs class.

```
                r.Changed += new EventHandler(r_Changed);
                r.Length = 10;
        }
        static void r_Changed(object sender, EventArgs e)
        {
                Rectangle r = (Rectangle)sender;
                Console.WriteLine(
                     "Value Changed: Length = {0}",
                     r.Length);
        }
    }
```

**TAKE NOTE** ✱

The code in the r_
Changed method uses a
cast operator to convert
an object data type to
the Rectangle data type.
Casting is explained
later in this lesson, in
the section entitled
"Casting Between
Types."

3. Select **Debug > Start Without Debugging.** A console window will pop up to display that the value of the Length property is changed.

4. SAVE your project.

**PAUSE.** Leave the project open to use in the next exercise.

In the example you just completed, the Rectangle class defines a Changed event that is invoked when the Length property of the Rectangle object is changed. The delegate of the Changed event is of EventHandler type. In the Rectangle class, the event Changed is invoked when the set accessor of the Length property is called.

You subscribe to the Changed event inside the Main method by attaching the r_Changed method as an event handler for the event by using the following code:

r.Changed += new EventHandler(r_Changed);

The signature of the r_Changed method matches the requirements of the EventHandler delegate. The r_Changed method is invoked as soon as you set the value of Length property in the Main method.

The above code uses the += operator rather than the simple assignment operator (=) to attach the event handler. By using the += operator, you make sure that this event handler will be added to a list of event handlers already attached with the event. This technique allows you have multiple event handlers that may respond to an event. If you use the assignment operator (=) to assign the new event handler, it will override any existing event handler that is attached to the event, and as a result, the newly attached event handler will be only one that is fired when the event is invoked.

## UNDERSTANDING NAMESPACES

A **namespace** allows you to organize code and create unique class names.

A namespace is a language element that allows you to organize code and create globally unique class names. Let's say you create a class of the name Widget. Chances are that some other company will also ship code that contains a class of the name Widget. In that case, how do you handle the ambiguity in names? The solution is to organize the code within a namespace. A common convention is to use the company name in the namespace. For example, you could do the following:

```
namespace CompanyA
{
    public class Widget { ... }
}
```

and

```
namespace CompanyB
{
    public class Widget { ... }
}
```

Here, the class from the namespace CompanyA can be uniquely referred to by its fully qualified class name CompanyA.Widget, whereas the other Widget can be uniquely identified as CompanyB.Widget.

The .NET Framework uses namespaces liberally to organize all its classes. For example, the System namespace groups all the fundamental classes. The System.Data namespace organizes classes for data access. Similarly, the System.Web namespace is used for Web-related classes.

Of course, with the use of namespaces, you might end up getting really long fully qualified class names that may result in verbose programs and a lot of typing. C# solves this inconvenience via the using directive. You can use the using directive at the top of the class file like this:

```
using System.Text;
```

Once you have included the using directive for a namespace, you don't need to fully qualify classes from that namespace in the file.

## UNDERSTANDING STATIC MEMBERS

*Static members* belong to a class itself rather than individual objects.

The class members discussed so far in this section (e.g., data fields, methods, and properties) all operate on individual objects. Such members are called as instance members because they can be used only after an instance of a class is created. In contrast, the *static* keyword is used to declare members that do not belong to individual objects but to a class itself. Such class members are called as static members. One common example of a static member is the familiar Main method that serves as the entry point for your program.

 ## CREATE STATIC MEMBERS

**USE** the project you saved in the previous exercise. Then, perform the following steps:

1. Modify the code of class Rectangle as shown below:

```
class Rectangle
{
    public static string ShapeName
    {
        get { return "Rectangle"; }
    }
    public double Length { get; set; }
    public double Width { get; set; }
    public double GetArea()
    {
        return this.Length * this.Width;
    }
}
```

2. Modify the code of the Program class to the following:

```
class Program
{
    static void Main(string[] args)
    {
        Rectangle rect = new Rectangle
            { Length = 10.0, Width = 20.0 };
        Console.WriteLine("Shape Name: {0}, Area: {1}",
            Rectangle.ShapeName,
            rect.GetArea());
    }
}
```

3. Select **Debug > Start Without Debugging**. A console window will pop up to display the name and area of the shape.

4. SAVE your project.

**PAUSE.** Leave the project open to use in the next exercise.

When an instance of a class is created, a separate copy is created for each instance field, but only one copy of a static field is shared by all instances.

**CERTIFICATION READY**
Do you understand the fundamentals of classes?
2.1

A static member cannot be referenced through an instance object. Instead, a static member is referenced through the class name (such as Rectangle.ShapeName in the above exercise). Note that it is not possible to use the *this* keyword reference with a static method or property because the *this* keyword can only be used to access instance objects.

# Understanding Values and References

**THE BOTTOM LINE**

A value type directly stores a value, whereas a reference type only stores a reference to an actual value.

A *value type* directly stores data within its memory. *Reference types*, on the other hand, store only a reference to a memory location; here, the actual data is stored at the memory location being referred to. Most built-in elementary data types (such as bool, int, char, double, etc.) are value types. User-defined data types created by using the keyword struct are value types as well. Reference types include the types created by using the keywords object, string, interface, delegate, and class.

## Understanding Structs

The keyword *struct* is used to create user-defined types that consist of small groups of related fields. Structs are value types—as opposed to classes, which are reference types.

Structs are defined by using the keyword struct, as shown below:

```
public struct Point
{
    public double X, Y;
}
```

Structs can contain most of the elements that classes can contain, such as constructors, methods, properties, etc. However, as you'll learn in the next section, structs are value types,

**TAKE NOTE** *

Structs are mostly used to create simple types. If you find yourself creating a very complex struct, you should consider using a class instead.

whereas classes are reference types. Unlike a class, a struct cannot inherit from another class or struct.

## Understanding Memory Allocation

After you enter a value or text into a cell, you can modify it in a number of ways. In particular, you can remove the contents completely, enter a different value to replace what was there, or alter what you have entered.

A good way to understand how value types differ from reference types is to visualize how each of them is represented in memory. Figure 2-1 shows how value types are created in memory. When you create a variable of type int, for instance, a named memory location is created that you can use to store a value of type int. Initially, when you don't explicitly assign a value, the default value of the data type (for int, the default value is 0) is stored in the memory location. Then, when an assignment is made, the memory address identified by the variable name is updated with the new value (10 in the case of the assignment in Figure 2-1).

**Figure 2-1**

Visualizing a value type in memory

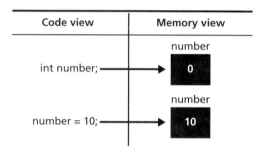

Now, take a look at Figure 2-2, which shows a reference type—specifically, the string data type. When you create a variable of type string, a memory location is created that will be identified by this name. However, this memory location will not contain the content of the string. Rather, this variable will store the memory address (a reference) of the location where the string is actually stored.

**Figure 2-2**

Visualizing a reference type in memory

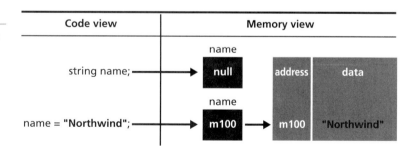

Initially, when no value is assigned, the variable will have the value of null (a null reference; in other words, this variable does not refer to a valid memory address). Then, in the next statement, when you say:

name = "Northwind";

the string "Northwind" is created at a particular memory location (to keep things simple, let's say the memory address is m100), and that memory address is stored in the variable name. Later, when it is time to retrieve the value of the variable name, the runtime will know that its contents are not stored in the variable itself, but rather at the memory location pointed to by the variable.

 ## COPY VALUE AND REFERENCE TYPES

**USE** the project you saved in the previous exercise to complete the steps below:

1. Add the following code after the Rectangle class definition to create a Point struct:

```
struct Point
{
    public double X, Y;
}
```

2. Modify the code of the Main method as shown below:

```
static void Main(string[] args)
{
    Point p1 = new Point();
    p1.X = 10;
    p1.Y = 20;
    Point p2 = p1;
    p2.X = 100;
    Console.WriteLine("p1.X = {0}", p1.X);
    Rectangle rect1 = new Rectangle
        { Length = 10.0, Width = 20.0 };
    Rectangle rect2 = rect1;
    rect2.Length = 100.0;
    Console.WriteLine("rect1.Length = {0}",
        rect1.Length);
}
```

3. Select **Debug > Start Without Debugging**. A console window will pop up to display the values for p1.X and rect1.Length.

4. SAVE your project.

**PAUSE.** Leave the project open to use in the next exercise.

Here, the first part of the program creates a copy of the value type Point, and the second half creates a copy of the reference type Rectangle.

Let's start by analyzing how the copy of a value type is made. To begin, when the following statement is executed, a new variable p2 is created in memory, and its contents are copied from the variable p1:

Point p2 = p1;

After this statement is executed, the variable p2 is created, and the content of variable p1 is copied to variable p2. Both p1 and p2 have their own set of values available in their respective memory locations. So, when the following statement is executed:

p2.X = 100;

it only affects the value of X corresponding to the memory location of variable p2. The value of X for variable p1 remains unaffected.

---

**TAKE NOTE*** 

It is possible to create a struct without using the new operator. You can simply say

Point p1;

to create a variable of the struct type.

---

**TAKE NOTE***

When you copy a reference type variable to another variable of the same type, only the references are copied. As a result, after the copy, both variables will point to the same object.

Now, let's analyze how the copy works between reference types. In this case, when the following statement is executed, a new variable rect2 is created, and just as before, the contents of rect1 are copied into the memory location of rect2:

```
Rectangle rect2 = rect1;
```

However, because the class Rectangle is a reference type, the content of variable rect1 is actually a reference to a memory location that holds a Rectangle object. So, after the above initialization, both rect1 and rect2 point to the same memory location and in turn the same Rectangle object. In other words, there is only one rectangle object in memory, and both rect1 and rect2 are referring to it. The next statement modifies the Length of that rectangle object:

```
rect2.Length = 100.0;
```

**CERTIFICATION READY**
Do you understand
data types and memory
allocation?
1.1

This statement references the memory location pointed to by rect2 (which happens to be the same memory location pointed to by rect1) and modifies the Length of the Rectangle object. Now, if you attempt to reference the same memory location via the rect1 object, you get the modified object and the following code displays the value "rect1.Length = 100":

```
Console.WriteLine("rect1.Length = {0}",
    rect1.Length);
```

---

**+ MORE INFORMATION**

Objects are always allocated memory on the heap. The heap is the memory available to a program at runtime for dynamic memory allocation. In contrast, some data items can be created on the execution stack or the call stack. Items created on the stack are the method parameters and the local variables declared within a method. The stack memory is reclaimed when the stack unwinds (when a method returns, for example). The memory allocated in the heap is automatically reclaimed by the garbage collector when the objects are not in use any more (i.e., no other objects are holding a reference to them).

---

# ■ Understanding Encapsulation

**THE BOTTOM LINE**  *Encapsulation* is an information-hiding mechanism that makes code easy to maintain and understand.

Encapsulation is a mechanism to restrict access to a class or class members in order to hide design decisions that are likely to change. Encapsulation gives class designers the flexibility to change a section of code when needed without changing all the other code that makes use of that code. Also, when you hide information, you hide the complexity associated with it. As a result, with the help of encapsulation, you can write code that is easier to understand and maintain.

In the previous exercises, you saw encapsulation at work when you declared the data members as private and enforced data-field initialization via a constructor. Because the data members are hidden from the users of the class, the developer of the Rectangle class can change the names of the data fields without requiring any changes in the calling code.

Properties offer a great way to encapsulate data fields along with any accompanying logic. Also, access modifiers such as private and public allow you to control the level of access for a class member or for the class itself.

In this section, you'll learn more about access modifiers and how they work.

## Understanding Access Modifiers

TAKE NOTE*

You should use the most restrictive access level that makes sense for a type member.

*Access modifiers* control where a type or type member can be used.

All types and type members have an access level that specifies where that class or its members can be used in your code. The access level can be set using one of the access modifiers specified in Table 2-1.

**Table 2-1**

Access Modifiers

| Access modifier | Description |
|---|---|
| public | Access is not restricted. |
| private | Access is restricted to the containing class. |
| protected | Access is restricted to the containing class and to any class that is derived directly or indirectly from the containing class. (You'll learn more about derived classes later in this lesson, in the section entitled "Understanding Inheritance.") |
| internal | Access is restricted to the code in the same assembly. |
| protected internal | A combination of protected **and** internal—that is, access is restricted to any code in the same assembly and only to derived classes in another assembly. |

TAKE NOTE* When C# code is compiled, the output executable code contained within a .dll or an .exe file is also called as an *assembly*. An assembly is a unit of executable code that can be independently versioned and installed.

**CERTIFICATION READY**
Do you understand encapsulation?
2.4

Access modifiers are not allowed in namespace declarations; public access is implied for namespaces. The top-level classes (declared directly under a namespace) can be only public or internal. The internal access modifier is the default for a class if no access modifier is specified. (For instance, the class Rectangle defined in the previous exercise defaults to having an internal access.) The accessibility of a nested class may not be less restrictive than the accessibility of the containing class.

# ■ Understanding Inheritance

**THE BOTTOM LINE**

Inheritance is a feature of object-oriented programming that allows you to develop a class once, and then reuse that code over and over as the basis of new classes. *Inheritance* enables you to create new classes that reuse, extend, and modify the functionality defined in existing classes. The class that inherits the functionality is called a *derived class*, and the class whose functionality is inherited is called a *base class*. A derived class inherits all the functionality of the base class and can also define additional features that make it different from the base class.

Say that we want to create a set of classes that describes polygons such as rectangles or triangles. These classes will have some common properties, such as width and length. For this case, you can create a base class Polygon with the Width and Length properties, and the derived classes Rectangle and Triangle will inherit these properties while providing their own functionality. The following exercise explains this concept in more detail.

 **CREATE DERIVED CLASSES**

**USE** the project you saved in the previous exercise to perform the following actions:

1. Add a new class named Polygon as shown below:

```
class Polygon
{
    public double Length { get; protected set; }
    public double Width { get; protected set; }
}
```

2. Modify the Rectangle class as shown below:

```
class Rectangle: Polygon
{
    public Rectangle(double length, double width)
    {
        Length = length;
        Width = width;
    }
    public double GetArea()
    {
        return Width * Length;
    }
}
```

3. Now, modify the code of the Main method as shown below:

```
static void Main(string[] args)
{
    Rectangle rect = new Rectangle(10, 20);
    Console.WriteLine(
        "Width={0}, Length={1}, Area = {2}",
        rect.Width, rect.Length, rect.GetArea());
}
```

4. Select **Debug > Start Without Debugging**. A console window will pop up to display the width, length, and the area of the rectangle.

5. SAVE your project.

**PAUSE.** Leave the project open to use in the next exercise.

To define a derived class, you put a colon after the derived class name, followed by the name of the base class. Here, the Polygon class is the base class for the Rectangle class.

The properties Length and Width in the Polygon class are declared with a protected access modifier for the set accessor. This means that access to the set accessor is available only inside the Polygon class and its derived classes. You can still get the value of the Length and Width properties in the Main method, but you'll get an error if you attempt to assign a value to these properties.

The Rectangle class inherits all the non-private data and behavior of the Polygon class. In addition, the Rectangle class defines additional functionality (GetArea method) that is not available in the base class.

## Understanding Abstract and Sealed Classes

The *abstract classes* provide a common definition of a base class that can be shared by multiple derived classes. The *sealed classes*, on the other hand, provide complete functionality but cannot be used as base classes.

In the previous exercise, you defined a GetArea method on the Rectangle class. Suppose you want to create another class, Triangle, that is of the Polygon type. Here, you'll need a GetArea method in the Triangle class that will calculate a triangle's area.

Often, base classes act as the repository of common functionality. In the case of Polygon, the polygon itself won't know how to calculate the area without knowledge of the shape type. But in general, we can expect all classes of the Polygon type to be able to calculate their area. Such expectations can be rolled over to the base class with the help of an abstract keyword.

### ⊙ CREATE ABSTRACT CLASSES

**USE** the project you saved in the previous exercise, and perform the following steps.

1. Modify the Polygon class as shown below:

```
abstract class Polygon
{
    public double Length { get; protected set; }
    public double Width { get; protected set; }
    abstract public double GetArea();
}
```

2. Modify the Rectangle class as shown below:

```
class Rectangle: Polygon
{
    public Rectangle(double length, double width)
    {
        Length = length;
        Width = width;
    }
    public override double GetArea()
    {
        return Width * Length;
    }
}
```

3. Note that no modification to the Main method is needed.
4. Select **Debug > Start Without Debugging**. A console window will pop up to display the width, length, and the area of the rectangle.
5. SAVE your project.

**PAUSE.** Leave the project open to use in the next exercise.

This version of the Polygon class defines a method named GetArea. The main reason for including this method in the base class is that now the base class can provide a common template of functionality for the derived classes. But, as we discussed, the Polygon base class doesn't know enough to calculate the area of the shape. This situation can be handled by marking the method as abstract. An abstract method provides a definition but does not offer any implementation (the method body). If any of the members of a class are abstract, the class itself needs to be marked as abstract. An abstract class cannot be instantiated.

Derived classes can provide an implementation of an abstract class to create a concrete class (a non-abstract class). The derived classes can offer an implementation of an abstract method by overriding it in a derived class. For example, the Rectangle class overrides the abstract GetArea method of the base class and provides a full implementation. As a result, the Rectangle class is no longer an abstract class and can be instantiated directly.

Sealed classes, on the other hand, are defined when your implementation is complete and you do not want a class to be inherited. A sealed class can be created by using the keyword *sealed*, as in the following example:

```
sealed class Rectangle: Polygon
{
    // class members here
}
```

Because Rectangle is a sealed class, it cannot be a used as a base class. It is also possible to mark selected class members as sealed to avoid them being overridden in a derived class. For example, you could say:

```
sealed public override double GetArea()
{
    return Width * Length;
}
```

This declaration ensures that the method GetArea cannot be overridden in a derived class.

## Inheriting from the Object Class

The Object class is the ultimate base class of all the classes in the .NET Framework.

All classes in the .NET Framework inherit either directly or indirectly from the Object class. For example, when you declared the following class earlier in this lesson:

```
class Polygon
{
    public double Length { get; protected set; }
    public double Width { get; protected set; }
}
```

it was functionally equivalent to the following declaration:

```
class Polygon: Object
{
    public double Length { get; protected set; }
    public double Width { get; protected set; }
}
```

However, you are not required to declare the Polygon class in the latter way because inheritance from the Object class is implicitly assumed. As part of this inheritance, a derived class can override the methods of the Object class. Two of the most common methods for doing this are as follows:

- **Equals:** Supports comparison between two objects, and returns true if the two objects have the same value.
- **ToString:** Returns a string representation of the class. By default, it returns the full name of the class. It is often useful to override this method so that it returns a string representation of the current state of the object.

The following example shows how you can override the ToString method in the Rectangle class:

```
class Rectangle: Polygon

{
    public Rectangle(double length, double width)
    {
        Length = length;
        Width = width;
    }
    public override double GetArea()
    {
        return Width * Length;
    }
    public override string ToString()
    {
        return String.Format(
            "Width = {0}, Length = {1}",
            Width, Length);
    }

}
```

## Casting between Types

In C#, the runtime allows you to *cast* an object to any of its base types.

Derived classes have an "is-a" relationship with their base class. For example, we can say that the Rectangle is a Polygon. Thus, an object of the Rectangle class has effectively two data types in this case: the object is a Rectangle, and the object is also a Polygon.

In C#, the runtime allows you to cast an object to its class or to any of its base classes. For example, you can say:

```
Polygon p = new Rectangle(10, 20);
```

Here, a new Rectangle object is created and is cast to its base type Polygon. C# doesn't require any special syntax to do this, because cast to base type is considered a safe conversion.

Casting is also possible the other way round. For example, you can say:

Object o = new Rectangle(10, 20);

...

Rectangle r = (Rectangle) o;

Here, a Rectangle object is first assigned to an Object (the ultimate base class), and the resultant object is then cast back as a Rectangle. When the latter assignment happens, an explicit cast is required because you are converting a more general object to a less general object. The runtime checks whether the value of the variable o is compatible with the Rectangle class. If, at execution time, the value of o is not compatible with the Rectangle class, the runtime throws a System.InvalidCastException.

## USING THE IS OPERATOR

To avoid runtime errors such as the InvalidCastException, the *is* operator can be used to check whether the cast is allowed before actually performing the cast, as in this example:

if (o is Rectangle)

{

Rectangle r = (Rectangle) o;

}

Here, the runtime checks the value of the object o. Then, the cast statement is only executed if o contains a Rectangle object.

## USING THE AS OPERATOR

Another useful cast operator is the *as* operator. The as operator is similar to the cast operation but, in the case of as, if the type conversion is not possible, null is returned instead of raising an exception. For example, consider the following code:

Rectangle r = o as Rectangle;

if (r != null)

{

    // do something

}

If, at runtime, it is not possible to cast the value of variable o to a rectangle, a value of null is assigned to the variable r. No exceptions will be raised.

**TAKE NOTE***

If you are using the as operator to convert a type, the is operator check is not necessary. You can simply check the return value from as against null.

**CERTIFICATION READY**
Do you understand inheritance?
2.2

# ■ Understanding Polymorphism

THE BOTTOM LINE

*Polymorphism* is the ability of derived classes to share common functionality with base classes but still define their own unique behavior.

You are developing an application that allows users to work with different kind of polygons. You have a collection that contains several types of polygons, such as a rectangle, a triangle, and a square. Each polygon provides you with its own implementation of the Draw method. When you work with this collection, you don't necessarily know exactly which shape you are working with, but you would like the correct Draw method to be invoked each time. Polymorphism enables you to do exactly this.

Polymorphism allows the objects of a derived class to be treated at runtime as objects of the base class. When a method is invoked at runtime, its exact type is identified, and the appropriate method is invoked from the derived class.

 **USE POLYMORPHISM**

**USE** the project you saved in the previous exercise to carry out the following steps:

1. Modify the Polygon class as shown below:

```
class Polygon
{
    public virtual void Draw()
    {
        Console.WriteLine("Drawing: Polygon");
    }
}
```

2. Modify the Rectangle class as shown below:

```
class Rectangle: Polygon
{
    public override void Draw()
    {
        Console.WriteLine("Drawing: Rectangle");
    }
}
```

3. Add a new class called Triangle, as shown below:

```
class Triangle: Polygon
{
    public override void Draw()
    {
        Console.WriteLine("Drawing: Triangle");
    }
}
```

4. Modify the Main method as follows:

```
static void Main(string[] args)
{
    List<Polygon> polygons = new List<Polygon>();
    polygons.Add(new Polygon());
    polygons.Add(new Rectangle());
    polygons.Add(new Triangle());
```

```
        foreach (Polygon p in polygons)
        {
            p.Draw();
        }
    }
```

5. Select **Debug > Start Without Debugging**. A console window will pop up to display the drawing message for each polygon.

6. SAVE your project.

**PAUSE.** Leave the project open to use in the next exercise.

In this exercise, the definitions of the Polygon and the Rectangle class are simplified to emphasize the concept of polymorphism. The base class provides a single Draw method. The important thing to note here is the keyword *virtual*. This keyword allows the derived classes to override the method.

Both the Rectangle and Triangle classes override the base class Draw method with their own definition by using the *override* keyword. When executed, the Main method generates the following output:

Drawing: Polygon

Drawing: Rectangle

Drawing: Triangle

The List<Polygon> data type is capable of storing a collection of objects that are of type Polygon or types that derive from Polygon. The foreach loop is iterating over a collection of Polygon objects. The underlying type of the first object is Polygon, but the second and third objects in the collection are actually Rectangle and Triangle objects that just happen to be cast as Polygons. The runtime will look at the actual underlying type and invoke the overridden method from the derived class. That's the reason why the derived class version of the Draw method is called for both Rectangle and Triangle objects.

## Understanding the Override and New Keywords

The *override* keyword replaces a base class member in a derived class. The *new* keyword creates a new member of the same name in the derived class and hides the base class implementation.

When a base class defines a virtual member, the derived class has two options for handling it—specifically, the derived class can use either the *override* keyword or the *new* keyword. The override keyword takes priority over the base-class definition of the member. Here, the object of the derived class will call the overridden member instead of the base-class member.

In comparison, if the new keyword is used, a new definition of the member is created and the base-class member is hidden. However, if the derived class is cast to an instance of the base class, the hidden members of the class can still be called.

**TAKE NOTE** ✱

If the method in the derived class is not preceded by the new keyword or the override keyword, the compiler will issue a warning, and the method will behave as if the new keyword were present.

To better understand these concepts, modify the Triangle method from the previous exercise to the following:

```
class Triangle: Polygon
{
    public new void Draw()
    {
        Console.WriteLine("Drawing: Triangle");
    }
}
```

Then, modify the code in the Main class to the following:

```
Triangle t = new Triangle();
t.Draw();
Polygon p = t;
p.Draw();
```

The program will produce the following output:

Drawing: Triangle

Drawing: Polygon

Here, when the Draw method is directly invoked on the object of the derived class, the new version of the method is used. However, if the method is executed when the derived class is cast as a base class, the hidden base-class version of the Draw method is executed.

**CERTIFICATION READY**
Do you understand polymorphism?
2.3

**TAKE NOTE** ✱  The System.Object class provides a ToString method. By convention, you should use this method to return the human-readable representation for a class. When you create your types, it is good practice to override this method to return readable information about the objects.

# ■ Understanding Interfaces

**THE BOTTOM LINE**  *Interfaces* are used to establish contracts through which objects can interact with each other without knowing the implementation details.

**TAKE NOTE** ✱

By convention, all interfaces defined in the .NET Framework begin with a capital I. Although you are free to name your interfaces as you wish, it is best to follow the Framework convention.

Interfaces are defined by using the *interface* keyword. An interface definition consists of a set of signatures for methods, properties, delegates, events, or indexers. An interface definition cannot consist of any data fields or any implementation details such as method bodies.

A common interface defined in the System namespace is the IComparable namespace. This is a simple interface defined as follows:

```
interface IComparable
{
    int CompareTo(object obj);
}
```

The IComparable interface has a single method (CompareTo) that accepts an object and returns an int. The return value of this method indicates the result of comparing the given parameter with the current object. According to the documentation of the CompareTo method:

- If the instance is equal to the parameter, CompareTo returns 0.
- If the parameter value is less than the instance or if the parameter is null, then a positive value is returned.
- If the parameter value is greater than the instance, then a negative value is returned.
- If the parameter is not of the compatible type, then an ArgumentException is thrown.

How does IComparable decide how to compare two Rectangle objects or two Employee objects? It doesn't. The classes that are interested in such comparisons must implement the IComparable interface by providing a method body for the CompareTo method. Each class that implements IComparable is free to provide its own custom comparison logic inside the CompareTo method.

 **USE THE ICOMPARABLE INTERFACE**

**USE** the project you saved in the previous exercise to carry out the following steps:

1. Modify the Rectangle class as shown below:

```
class Rectangle: Polygon, IComparable
{
    public double Length { get; set; }
    public double Width { get; set; }
    public override void Draw()
{
        Console.WriteLine("Drawing: Rectangle");
    }
    public double GetArea()
    {
        return Length * Width;
    }
    public int CompareTo(object obj)
    {
        if (obj == null)
            return 1;

        if (!(obj is Rectangle))
            throw new ArgumentException();

        Rectangle target = (Rectangle)obj;
        double diff = this.GetArea() - target.GetArea();
```

```
              if (diff == 0)
                  return 0;
              else if (diff > 0)
                  return 1;
              else return -1;
        }
   }
```

3. Then, modify the Main method as shown below:

```
static void Main(string[] args)
{
      Rectangle rect1 = new Rectangle
          { Length = 10, Width = 20 };
      Rectangle rect2 = new Rectangle
          { Length = 100, Width = 200 };

      Console.WriteLine(rect1.CompareTo(rect2));
}
```

4. Select **Debug > Start Without Debugging**. A console window will pop up and display the value –1 because the area of rect1 is less than the area of rect2.

5. SAVE your project.

Here, the class Rectangle both derives from the Polygon class and implements the IComparable interface. A class that implements an interface must implement all the methods declared in that interface.

An interface is similar to an abstract class, but there are some noticeable differences. For one, an abstract class provides incomplete implementation, whereas an interface provides no implementation at all. A class can also implement multiple interfaces but is limited to inheriting from only a single base class.

So, how do you decide whether to use an abstract class or an interface? One way is to check whether an "is-a" relationship exists between the two concepts. For example, if an inheritance relationship exists between a SalariedEmployee and an Employee, then you can use an abstract class to standardize common functionality among derived classes. On the other hand, there is no "is-a" relationship between an Employee and the IComparable. Therefore, the comparison functionality is best implemented as an interface.

**CERTIFICATION READY**
Do you understand encapsulation?
2.4

## SKILL SUMMARY

**IN THIS LESSON, YOU LEARNED THE FOLLOWING:**

- Objected-oriented programming is a programming technique that makes use of objects. Objects are self-contained data structures that consist of properties, methods, and events. Properties specify the data represented by an object, methods specify an object's behavior, and events provide communication between the objects.
- A class is the template from which individual objects are created.
- Constructors are used to initialize the data members of an object.

- The *this* keyword can be used to access members from within constructors, instance methods, and the accessors of instance properties.
- Delegates are special types that are used to encapsulate a method with a specific signature.
- Events are a way for a class to notify other classes or objects when something of interest happens. The class that sends a notification is called the publisher of the event, and the class that receives the notification is called the subscriber of the event.
- Namespaces allow you to organize code and create unique class names.
- The *static* keyword is used to declare members that do not belong to individual objects but to a class itself.
- A value type directly stores a value, whereas a reference type only stores a reference to an actual value.
- The keyword *struct* is used to create user-defined types that consist of small groups of related fields. Structs are value types, whereas classes are reference types.
- Encapsulation is a mechanism to restrict access to a class or class members in order to hide design decisions that are likely to change. Encapsulation provides class designers with the flexibility to change a section of code as needed without changing all other code that makes use of that code.
- An access modifier specifies what region of the code will have access to a field. For example, a public access modifier does not limit access, but a private access modifier limits access within the class in which the field is defined.
- Inheritance enables you to create new classes that reuse, extend, and modify the functionality defined in existing classes. The class that inherits functionality is called a derived class, and the class whose functionality is inherited is called a base class.
- Polymorphism is the ability of derived classes to share common functionality with base classes but still define their own unique behavior.
- The *override* keyword replaces a base-class member in a derived class. The *new* keyword creates a new member with the same name in the derived class and hides the base-class implementation.

# ■ Knowledge Assessment

## Fill in the Blank

*Complete the following sentences by writing the correct word or words in the blanks provided.*

1. A(n) _____ is a blueprint of an object.

2. A class that does not provide a complete implementation must be declared with the keyword _____.

3. Classes that want to support comparison must implement the IComparable interface and then provide a body for the _____ method.

4. You can use the _____ operator to check whether it is legal to cast one type to another type.

5. Three main features of an object-oriented programming language are _____, _____, and _ _____.

6. You can use _____ to group related classes in order to reduce name collisions.

7. The _____ keyword refers to the current instance of a class.

8. A(n) _____ is a type that references a method.

9. A(n) _____ is a value type, whereas a(n) _____ is a reference type.

10. You can use the _____ keyword to declare a member that belongs to the class itself rather than to a specific object.

## Multiple Choice

*Circle the letter that corresponds to the best answer.*

1. You want to restrict the access for a method to the containing class or to a class that is derived from the containing class. Which access modifier should you use for this method?
   a. public
   b. private
   c. protected
   d. internal

2. In a class, you defined a method called Render. This method provides functionality to render bitmap files on the screen. You would like the derived classes to supersede this functionality to support the rendering of additional image formats. You also want the Render method of the derived classes to be executed even if a derived class is cast as the base class. Which keyword should you use with the definition of the Render method in the base class?
   a. abstract
   b. virtual
   c. new
   d. overrides

3. You defined a class AdvMath that defines advanced mathematical functionality. You do not want the functionality of this class to be inherited into derived classes. What keyword should you use to define the AdvMath class?
   a. sealed
   b. abstract
   c. private
   d. internal

4. You need to provide query functionality to several of your classes. Each class's algorithm for the query will likely be different. Also, not all the classes have an "is-a" relationship with each other. How should you support this functionality?
   a. Add the query functionality to a base class with the public access modifier
   b. Have all the classes inherit from an abstract base class and override the base-class method to provide their own query functionality
   c. Have all the classes inherit from a base class that provides the query functionality
   d. Create a common interface that is implemented by all the classes

5. Which of the following class elements should you use to define the behavior of a class?
   a. Method
   b. Property
   c. Event
   d. Delegate

6. You are writing code for a class named Product. You need to make sure that the data members of the class are initialized to their correct values as soon as you create an object of the Product class. The initialization code should be always executed. What should you do?
   a. Create a static method in the Product class to initialize data members
   b. Create a constructor in the Product class to initialize data members
   c. Create a static property in the Product class to initialize data members
   d. Create an event in the Product class to initialize data members

7. You are creating a new class named Square that is derived from the Polygon class. The Polygon class has the following code:

```
class Polygon
{
    public virtual void Draw()
    {
        // additional code . . .
    }
}
```

The Draw method in the Square class should provide new functionality but also hide the Polygon class implementation of the Draw method. Which code segment should you use to accomplish this?

a. 
```
class Square: Polygon
{
    public override void Draw()
    {
        // additional code . . .
    }
}
```

b. 
```
class Square: Polygon
{
    public new void Draw()
    {
        // additional code . . .
    }
}
```

c. 
```
class Square: Polygon
{
    public virtual void Draw()
    {
        // additional code . . .
    }
}
```

**d.** class Square: Polygon

```
{
        public static void Draw()
        {
            // additional code . . .
        }
}
```

8. You are creating a new class named Rectangle. You write the following code:

```
class Rectangle: IComparable
{
        public double Length { get; set; }
        public double Width { get; set; }
        public double GetArea()
        {
                return Length * Width;
        }
         public int CompareTo(object obj)
         {
            // to be completed
         }
}
```

You need to complete the definition of the CompareTo method to enable comparison of the Rectangle objects. Which of the following codes should you write?

**a.** public int CompareTo(object obj)

```
{
        Rectangle target = (Rectangle)obj;
        double diff = this.GetArea() − target.GetArea();

        if (diff == 0)
            return 0;
        else if (diff > 0)
            return 1;
        else return −1;
}
```

**b.** public int CompareTo(object obj)

```
{
        Rectangle target = (Rectangle)obj;
        double diff = this.GetArea() − target.GetArea();
        if (diff == 0)
            return 1;
        else if (diff > 0)
            return −1;
        else return 0;
}
```

```
c. public int CompareTo(object obj)
   {
        Rectangle target = (Rectangle)obj;
        if (this == target)
            return 0;
        else if (this > target)
            return 1;
        else return -1;
   }

d. public int CompareTo(object obj)
   {
        Rectangle target = (Rectangle)obj;
        if (this == target)
            return 1;
        else if (this > target)
            return -1;
        else return 0;
   }
```

9. You are writing code for a new method named Process:

```
void Process(object o)
{

}
```

The code receives a parameter of type object. You need to cast this object into the type Rectangle. At times, the value of o that is passed to the method might not be a valid Rectangle value. You need to make sure that the code does not generate any System. InvalidCastException errors while doing the conversions. Which of the following lines of code should you use inside the Process method to accomplish this goal?

a. Rectangle r = (Rectangle) o;

b. Rectangle r = o as Rectangle;

c. Rectangle r = o is Rectangle;

d. Rectangle r = (o != null) ? o as rectangle: (Rectangle) o;

10. You are writing code to handle events in your program. You define a delegate named RectangleHandler like this:

```
public delegate void RectangleHandler(Rectangle rect);
```

You also create a variable of the RectangleHandler type as follows:

```
RectangleHandler handler;
```

Later in the program, you need to add a method named DisplayArea to the method invocation list of the handler variable. The signature of the DisplayArea method matches the signature of the RectangleHandler method. Any code that you write should not affect any existing event-handling code. Given this restriction, which of the following codes should you write?

a. handler = new RectangleHandler(DisplayArea);

b. handler = DisplayArea;

c. handler += DisplayArea;

d. handler -= DisplayArea;

# ■ Competency Assessment

## Scenario 2-1: Creating Properties

You need to create a class named Product that represents a product. The class has a single property named Name. Users of the Product class should be able to get as well as set the value of the Name property. However, any attempt to set the value of Name to an empty string or a null value should raise an exception. Also, users of the Product class should not be able to access any other data members of the Product class. How will you create such a class?

## Scenario 2-2: Creating a Struct

You are developing a game that needs to represent the location of a target in three-dimensional space. The location is identified by the three integer values denoted x, y, and z. You will create thousands of these data structures in your program, and you need a lightweight, efficient way to store this data in memory. Also, it is unlikely that you will need to inherit any other types from this location type. How should you represent the location in your program?

# ■ Proficiency Assessment

## Scenario 2-1: Overriding the ToString Method

Say you are writing code for a Product class. The Product class contains the name and price of a product. You need to override the base class (System.Object) method ToString to provide information about the objects of the product class to the calling code. What code do you need to write for the Product class in order to meet this requirement?

## Scenario 2-2: Creating and Handling Events

Imagine that you are writing code for creating and handling events in your program. The class SampleClass needs to implement the following interface:

```
public delegate void SampleDelegate();
public interface ISampleEvents
{
    event SampleDelegate SampleEvent;
    void Invoke();
}
```

You need to write code for the SampleClass and for a test method that creates an instance of the SampleClass and invokes the event. What code should you write?

# Understanding General Software Development

## LESSON SKILL MATRIX

| SKILLS/CONCEPTS | MTA EXAM OBJECTIVE | MTA EXAM OBJECTIVE NUMBER |
|---|---|---|
| Understanding Application Lifecycle Management | Understand application lifecycle management. | 3.1 |
| Understanding Testing | Understand application lifecycle management. | 3.1 |
| Understanding Data Structures | Understand algorithms and data structures. | 3.3 |
| Understanding Sorting Algorithms | Understand algorithms and data structures. | 3.3 |

### KEY TERMS

acceptance testing

application lifecycle management (ALM)

arrays

black-box testing

Bubblesort

data structures

design process

integration testing

linked list

QuickSort

queue

regression testing

release management

requirements analysis

software development

software testing

sorting algorithms

stack

system testing

unit testing

white-box testing

You are a software developer for the Northwind Corporation. You work as part of a team to develop computer programs that solve complex business problems. As a developer, you need to be aware of the different phases of the application lifecycle because you play an important role in multiple parts of this cycle. For instance, not only do you participate in the design and development portions of the cycle, but you often need to interact with the software testing team during the testing portion of the cycle. Sometimes, you even engage in testing yourself, so you need to have a general understanding of this process.

When you develop software, you use various types of data structures and algorithms. Therefore, you need to know which data structure to use for the task at hand and what the performance implications of your choice are. You should also have a general understanding of various sorting methods.

## ■ Understanding Application Lifecycle Management

 **THE BOTTOM LINE**

*Application lifecycle management (ALM)* is the set of activities that revolve around a new software product, from its inception to when the product matures and perhaps retires.

Developing a software application involves more than just writing the code. Various other activities also need to be performed in the right order to develop a successful application. Collectively, these activities are known as application lifecycle management (ALM). Some of the activities that are part of the ALM process are shown in Figure 3-1, including requirements, design, development, testing, delivery, and release management.

**Figure 3-1**

Application lifecycle management

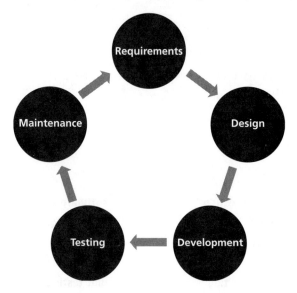

In this section, you'll learn about the different activities and roles involved in each stage of the ALM process.

The application lifecycle starts when the need for a new software application is identified. A business manager is usually the person who is the sponsor of the project. He or she analyzes the need, checks how the project fits with the overall strategy of the business, arranges the funding, and initiates the staffing process for the project.

A project manager is probably the first person hired by the business manager. The project manager is responsible for the overall execution of the project. His or her key responsibilities are to make sure that the project stays on budget and finishes on time. The project manager is also responsible for hiring team members and for facilitating cooperation within the team.

### Understanding Requirements Analysis

*Requirements analysis* is the process of determining the detailed business requirements for a new software system.

Requirements analysis is one of the most important steps in the application lifecycle. Precise, complete, well-documented requirements are critical to the success of the project. These requirements can be functional or nonfunctional. Functional requirements specify exactly what the system is designed to accomplish. In contrast, nonfunctional requirements are quality requirements such as scalability, security, reliability, and so on.

A business analyst is responsible for analyzing business needs and converting them into requirements that can be executed by the development team.

## Understanding the Design Process

> The *design process* is used to create plans, models, and architecture for how the software will be implemented.

The design process generates detailed technical specifications that will be used for developing the system. The output of the design process is a set of technical models and specifications that provide guidance to the developers and other team members during the software development activity. The output of the design process is more abstract than concrete. At this point, no real system exists that you can interact with.

Some of the most important participants in this stage of the ALM process include an architect and a user-experience designer:

- **Architect:** An architect designs the technical blueprint of the system. This includes identifying components and services, their behavior, and how they interact with each other and with the external world.
- **User-experience designer:** A user-experience designer creates the user experience of the system. This includes designing the user interface (UI) elements; designing navigation between various forms, screens, or pages; and so on.

## Understanding Software Development

> The *software development* activity involves implementing design by creating software code, databases, and other related content.

Software development is the portion of the ALM process in which the business requirements are implemented in working code based on the design that was created in the previous activity. At the end of this activity, you have concrete output in form of a software system with which users can interact.

Critical participants in software development include the following:

- **Developers:** Developers write code based on the requirements gathered by the business analyst, the architecture laid down by the architect, and the user experience developed by the user-experience designer.
- **Database administrators (DBAs):** DBAs are responsible for implementation and maintenance of the software's databases. DBAs also plan for data integrity, security, and speed.
- **Technical writers:** Technical writers develop the system manuals and help files that will be delivered along with the application.
- **Content developers:** Content developers are subject matter experts who develop the content for the system. For example, if the application is a movie review website, just deploying the website is not enough—you also need to make sure that the site has enough content to gather user interest.

### Understanding Software Testing

> *Software testing* verifies that the implementation matches the requirements of the system.

Software testing is used to assure the quality of the final product. Testing can identify possible gaps between the system expectations described in the requirements document and actual system behavior.

Among the most critical participants in the software testing activity are the testers who verify the working application to make sure that it satisfies the identified requirements. When these testers identify any defects in the application, they assign each defect to an appropriate person who can fix it. For example, a code defect would be assigned back to a developer so he or she could remedy the error.

### Understanding Release Management

> The *release management* activity is used to manage the deployment, delivery, and support of software releases.

Release management includes activities such as packaging and deploying the software, managing software defects, and managing software change requests.

Major players in the release management activity include the following individuals:

- **Release manager:** The release manager coordinates various teams and business units to ensure timely release of a software product.
- **Operation staff:** The operation staff members make sure that the system is delivered as promised. This could involve burning DVDs and shipping them as orders are received, or it could entail maintaining a Software as a Service (SaaS) system on an ongoing basis. Operation staff are also responsible for releasing any system updates (e.g., bug fixes or new features).
- **Technical support staff:** These staffers interact with customers and help solve their problems with the system. Technical support can generate valuable metrics about what areas of the system are most difficult for users and possibly need to be updated in the next version of the application.

**CERTIFICATION READY**
Do you understand application lifecycle management and its activities?
3.1

## ■ Understanding Testing

**THE BOTTOM LINE**
Software testing is the process of verifying software against its requirements. Testing takes place after most development work is completed.

As previously mentioned, software testing is the process of verifying that a software application works as expected and fulfills all its business and technical requirements. When there is a difference between the expected behavior and the actual behavior of the system, a software defect (or "bug") is logged and eventually passed on to an individual who is responsible for fixing it.

Software testing may involve both functional and nonfunctional testing. Functional testing relates to the functional requirements of the system, and it tests those features that make up the core functionality of the system. For example, testing whether users can add items to a shopping cart is an important part of functional testing for an e-commerce Web site. In comparison, nonfunctional testing involves testing software attributes that are not part of the core functionality but rather part of the software's nonfunctional requirements, such as scalability, usability, security.

**TAKE NOTE** *

It is important to note that the process of software testing can only *help* find defects—it cannot guarantee the absence of defects. Complex software has a huge number of possible execution paths and many parameters that can affect its behavior. It is not feasible and often not possible to test all the different situations that such software will encounter in a production environment.

## Understanding Testing Methods

Software testing *methods* are generally divided into two categories: white-box and black-box testing.

Traditionally, there are two broad approaches to software testing:

- *Black-box testing*
- *White-box testing*

Black-box testing treats the software as a black box, focusing solely on inputs and outputs. With this approach, any knowledge of internal system workings is not used during testing. In contrast, with white-box testing, testers use their knowledge of system internals when testing the system. For example, in white-box testing, the testers have access to the source code.

These two testing techniques complement each other. Black-box testing is mostly used to make sure a software application covers all its requirements. Meanwhile, white-box testing is used to make sure that each method or function has proper test cases available.

## Understanding Testing Levels

Testing is performed at various phases of the application development lifecycle. Different *testing levels* specify where in the lifecycle a particular test takes place, as well as what kind of test is being performed.

Testing levels are defined by where the testing takes place within the course of the software development lifecycle. Five distinct levels of testing exist:

- *Unit testing:* Unit testing verifies the functionality of a unit of code. For example, a unit test may assess whether a method returns the correct value. Unit testing is white-box testing, and it is frequently done by the developer who is writing the code. Unit testing often uses an automated tool that can simplify the development of cases and also keep track of whether a code modification causes any of the existing unit tests to fail. Visual Studio has built-in support for unit testing. You can also use open-source tools such as NUnit to automate unit tests for the .NET Framework code.
- *Integration testing:* Integration testing assesses the interface between software components. Integration testing can be performed incrementally as the components are being

developed, or it can be performed as a "big bang" when all the components are ready to work together. The former approach is preferred to the latter because it reduces risk and increases stakeholders' confidence as the system is being developed. Integration testing can also involve testing the component's interaction with an external system. For example, if a component relies on data from an external Web service, integration testing ensures that the component is working well with the external application.

- *System testing:* System testing is the overall testing of the software system. At this point, all the system components are developed and are working together and with any external systems.

- *Acceptance testing:* This level of testing is often performed by the customers themselves. There are generally two levels of acceptance testing prior to broad release of a product: alpha testing and beta testing. Alpha testing is performed by a limited group of users, and it is an opportunity to provide an early look at the product to the most important customers and gather feedback. Alpha releases may miss some features and generally lack many nonfunctional attributes such as performance. In the next level of testing, beta testing, you release the product to a wider audience of customers and solicit feedback. In terms of functionality, the beta release of the software is very close to the final release. However, the development teams might still be working on improving performance and fixing known defects.

- *Regression testing:* As the defects in a software application are reported and fixed, it is important to make sure that each new fix doesn't break anything that was previously working. This is where regression testing comes in handy. With every new fix, software testers usually run a battery of regression tests to make sure that each functionality that was already known to work correctly is still working.

## ■ Understanding Data Structures

**THE BOTTOM LINE**

*Data structures* are techniques for organizing and storing data in computer memory. How the data is stored affects how the data is retrieved and manipulated. Understanding a data structure involves not only understanding the storage pattern, but also knowing what methods are used to create, access, and manipulate the data structure.

Data structures are the building blocks of most computer programs, and they allow developers to implement complex functionality. Most programming frameworks provide built-in support for a variety of data structures and associated methods to manipulate these data structures. In this section, you will learn about several distinct types of data structures so that you are familiar with the general techniques for manipulating them.

### Understanding Arrays

An *array* is a collection of items stored in a contiguous memory location and addressed using one or more indices.

An array is a common data structure that represents a collection of items of a similar type. The items in an array are stored in contiguous memory locations. An array is a homogeneous data structure because the all the items of an array are of the same data type. Any array item can be directly accessed by using an index. In .NET Framework, array indexes are zero-based.

## INTERNAL REPRESENTATION

In the following code, the first statement creates an array variable, and the second statement initializes the variable with an array of four integers:

```
int[] numbers;
```

```
numbers = new int[4];
```

At first, the variable numbers are set to null because the array is not yet initialized. However, the second statement initializes the array by allocating a contiguous memory space big enough to store four integers in the memory heap. The starting address in the memory allocation is stored in the array variable *numbers*, as shown in Figure 3-2. All the array elements are initialized in this case with the value 0 because 0 is the default value for an integer.

**Figure 3-2**

Internal representation of an array data structure

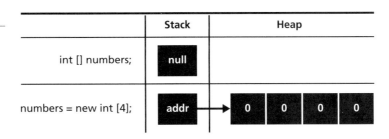

The variable numbers then acts as a reference to the memory location assigned to the array. The array name can be used to access each of the array items directly. In the .NET Framework, all arrays are zero-based—that is, the first item of the array is accessed using an index of numbers[0], the second item is accessed by numbers[1], and so on.

It is also possible to have multidimensional arrays. A two-dimensional array can be thought of as a table in which each cell is an array element and can be addressed using the numbers of the row and column to which it belongs. Both the row number and column number are indexed by zero. For example, the expression table[2, 3] would refer to an item in the third row and fourth column of an array by the name table.

## COMMON OPERATIONS

Arrays support the following operations:

- Allocation
- Access

To work with an array, you first allocate the memory by creating and initializing the array, as shown previously. Once the array is allocated, you can access any array element in any order you please by directly referring to its index. For example, the following code assigns a value of 10 to the fourth item of the array, and twice that value is then assigned to the variable calc:

```
number[3] = 10;
```

```
int calc = number[3] * 2;
```

## PERFORMANCE AND USAGE

The contents of an array are laid out as a contiguous block of memory and can be accessed directly by using the array index. Thus, reading from or writing to an array is extremely fast. However, arrays are limited by the requirements of homogeneity and fixed size. Although array size can be increased, doing so requires reallocation of all the array elements and is a time-consuming operation.

Arrays work best when the number of items in the collection is predetermined and fast, direct access to each item is required.

In the .NET Framework, you can use the ArrayList class to get around an array's requirements for homogeneity and fixed size. An ArrayList is a collection type that can hold items of any data type and dynamically expand when needed. However, an ArrayList is not as fast as an array.

## Understanding Queues

A *queue* is a collection of items in which the first item added to the collection is the first one to be removed.

The queue data structure mimics a real-life queue. In a queue, items are processed in the order in which they were added to the queue. In particular, items are always added at the end of the queue and removed from the front of the queue. This is also commonly known as first-in, first-out (FIFO) processing. The capacity of a queue is the number of items the queue can hold. However, as elements are added to the queue, the capacity is automatically increased. A queue is also a heterogeneous data structure, meaning that items in a queue can be of different data types.

## INTERNAL REPRESENTATION

In order to avoid excessive reallocation of memory space and allow easy management, a queue is often internally implemented as a circular array of objects, as shown in Figure 3-3.

**Figure 3-3**

Internal representation of a queue data structure

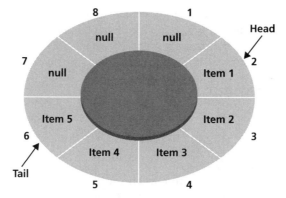

Within a queue, the head index points to the first item, and the tail index points to the last item. In Figure 3-3, for example, the head index points to location 2 on the queue. Because the queue is circular, as long as you can keep track of the head and tail pointers, it doesn't matter what location the queue starts from. When an item is removed, the head moves to the

A generic version of the Queue class is available as part of the System.Collections.Generic namespace. This generic version is used to create a queue of items that are of the same data type.

next item in the queue. When a new item is added, it always appears at the end of the queue, and the tail starts pointing to the newly added item. Any null slots in a queue (including the one depicted in Figure 3-3) are the empty spots that can be filled before the queue will require a memory reallocation.

The .NET Framework provides an implementation of the queue data structure as part of the Queue class in the System.Collections namespace. In programming languages that don't provide an implementation of a queue, you can write your own Queue class by using an array-like data structure and simulating the queue operations.

## COMMON OPERATIONS

A queue supports the following common operations:

- **Enqueue:** The enqueue operation first checks whether there is enough capacity available in the queue to add one more item. If capacity is available, the item is added to the tail end of the queue. If there is no space available in queue, the array is reallocated by a prespecified growth factor, and the new item is then added to the queue.
- **Dequeue:** The dequeue operation removes the current element at the head of the queue and sets the head to point to the next element.
- **Peek:** The peek operation allows you to look at the current item at the head position without actually removing it from the queue.
- **Contains:** The contains operation allows you to determine whether a particular item exists in the queue.

## PERFORMANCE AND USAGE

A queue is a special-purpose data structure that is best suited for an application in which you need to process items in the order they were received. Some examples may include print spoolers, messaging systems, and job schedulers. Unlike an array, a queue cannot be used to randomly access elements. Operations such as enqueue and dequeue actually add and remove the items from the queue.

## Understanding Stacks

A *stack* is a collection of items in which the last item added to the collection is the first one to be removed.

As opposed to a queue, a stack is a last-in, first-out (LIFO) data structure. Think of a stack as similar to a stack of dinner plates on a buffet table; here, the last plate to be added is also the first plate to be removed. The capacity of a stack refers to the number of items it can hold. However, as elements are added to a stack, the stack's capacity is automatically increased. A stack is a heterogeneous data structure, meaning that the items within it can be of different data types.

## INTERNAL REPRESENTATION

Like a queue, a stack is often implemented as a circular buffer in order to avoid excessive reallocation of memory space and permit easier management. A stack can be visualized just like the queue shown in Figure 3-3, except that the tail is now called the top of the stack and the head is now called the bottom of the stack.

**TAKE NOTE** *

A generic version of the Stack class is available as part of the System. Collections.Generic namespace. This generic version is used to create a stack of items that are of the same data type.

New items are always added to the top of a stack; when this happens, the top of the stack starts pointing to the newly added element. Items are also removed from the top of the stack, and when that happens, the top of the stack is adjusted to point to the next item in the stack.

The .NET Framework provides an implementation of the stack data structure as part of the Stack class in the System.Collections namespace. In programming languages that don't provide an implementation of the stack, you can write your own Stack class by using an array-like data structure and simulating the stack operations.

## COMMON OPERATIONS

A stack supports the following common operations:

- **Push:** The push operation first checks whether there is enough capacity available in the stack to add one more item. If capacity is available, the item is added to the top of the stack. If there is no space in the stack, the array is reallocated by a prespecified growth factor, and then the new item is added to the stack.
- **Pop:** The pop operation removes the element at the top of the stack and sets the top to point to the next element in the stack.
- **Peek:** The peek operation allows you to look at the current item at the top of the stack without actually removing it from the stack.
- **Contains:** The contains operation allows you to determine whether a particular item exists in the stack.

## PERFORMANCE AND USAGE

A stack is a special-purpose data structure that is best suited for applications in which you need to process items in last-in, first-out order. Stack are useful structures because of their applications in runtime memory management, expression evaluation, method-call tracking, etc. Unlike an array, a stack cannot be used to access elements randomly. Operations such as push and pop actually add and remove the items from the stack.

## Linked Lists

A *linked list* is a collection of nodes arranged so that each node contains a link to the next node in the sequence.

A linked list is a collection of nodes in which each node contains a reference (or link) to the next node in the sequence. Unlike an array, the items in a linked list need not be contiguous; therefore, a linked list does not require reallocation of memory space for the entire list when more items must be added.

### INTERNAL REPRESENTATION

In memory, a linked list can be visualized as a collection of nodes, as shown in Figure 3-4.

**Figure 3-4**

Internal representation of a single linked-list data structure

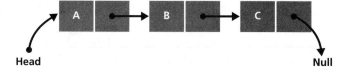

**Head**    **Null**

Each node in a linked list contains of two pieces of information: the data corresponding to the node, and the link to the next node. The first node of the list is called the head node. Using the link in the head node, you can get to the next node and continue traversing nodes until the final link is a null value. Often, the term *tail* is used to refer to the list pointed to by the head node—that is, it refers to everything after the head node. Thus, in Figure 3-4, the tail is the linked list starting from node B.

Several other implementations of linked lists may also be used depending on requirements. For instance, in a circular linked list, the last node in the list points back to the first node to create a circle. In contrast, in a doubly linked list, each node contains two links, as shown in Figure 3-5.

**Figure 3-5**

Internal representation of a doubly linked list data structure

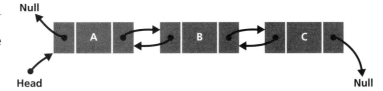

At each node of a doubly linked list, one link is a forward reference that points to the next node in the sequence, and the other link is a backward reference that points to the previous node in the sequence. As you can imagine, a doubly linked list is easy to traverse in either direction.

The .NET Framework provides a LinkedList class as part of the System.Collections.Generic namespace. This class implements a homogeneous doubly linked list of the specified data type. You can also write your own classes to implement a different kind of linked-list implementation.

## COMMON OPERATIONS

A linked list supports the following common operations:

- **Add:** Adding or inserting an item in a linked list is a matter of changing links, as shown in Figure 3-6. Say you want to insert a new node (with value Z) between the nodes with values A and B. First, you need to allocate memory for the new node and assign value Z

**Figure 3-6**

Adding a new node to a linked list

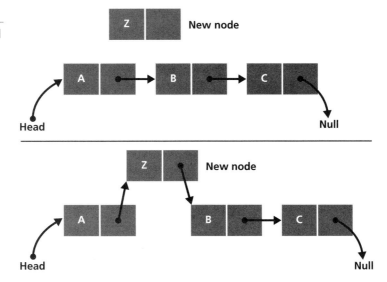

to the data section of the node. Next, you must copy the link section of node A to the link section of node Z so that node Z is pointing to node B. Finally, you must copy the address of the newly created node Z to the link section of node A so that node A starts pointing to node Z.

- **Remove:** Similar to the add operation, the remove or delete operation is also a matter of changing links. For example, to delete the third node in Figure 3-4, you would change the link for the second node to a null value. The third node will now be an unreferenced piece of memory, and it will eventually be returned to the pool of available memory.

- **Find:** The find operation finds a node with a given value in the linked list. To find a value, you generally start from the head node and check whether the value matches. If not, you follow the link to the next node and continue the find operation until you reach the end of the list, which happens when you encounter a null link.

### PERFORMANCE AND USAGE

A linked list does not allow random access to its items. The only way to get to an item is to start from the head node and follow the links from there. As a result, linked lists are slow at retrieving data. However, for insert and delete operations, linked lists are extremely fast, because insertion or deletion of a node involves simply changing a link. Linked lists also have no maximum capacity after which their contents need to be reallocated.

In fact, a linked list provides an alternative way to implement the queue and the stack data structures. If your requirements call for frequent access to data but you seldom need to insert or delete data, an array is the preferred implementation. If, however, your requirements call for frequent insert and delete operations, then a linked list may be a better implementation.

**CERTIFICATION READY**
Do you understand the common data structures?
3.2

## ■ Understanding Sorting Algorithms

↓ **THE BOTTOM LINE**

*Sorting algorithms*, such as BubbleSort and QuickSort, arrange items in a list in a particular order. Understanding sorting algorithms can help you understand, analyze, and compare different methods of problem solving.

Sorting algorithms are algorithms that arrange the items in a list in a certain order. For example, you can use a sorting algorithm to sort a list of students in ascending order of their last name. In the early days of data processing, sorting was an important problem that attracted a lot of research. These days, you can find basic sorting capabilities already built into most popular libraries and data structures. For example, in the .NET Framework, you can make use of the Array.Sort method to sort an array. However, it is still important to look at sorting as a way to understand problem solving and algorithm analysis.

In this section, you will take a look at two common sorting algorithms, BubbleSort and QuickSort.

### Understanding BubbleSort

The *BubbleSort* algorithm uses a series of comparison and swap operations to arrange the elements of a list in the correct order.

BubbleSort works by comparing two elements to check whether they are out of order; if they are, it swaps them. The algorithm continues to do this until the entire list is in the desired order. BubbleSort gets its name from the way the algorithm works: As the algorithm progresses, the smaller items are "bubbled" up.

Let's visualize BubbleSort with the help of an example. Say you want to arrange all the items in the following list in ascending order: (20, 30, 10, 40). These items should be arranged from smallest to largest. The BubbleSort algorithm attempts to solve this problem in one or more passes, with each pass completely scanning the list of items. If the algorithm encounters out-of-order elements, it swaps them. The algorithm finishes when it scans the whole list without swapping any elements. If there were no swaps, then none of the elements were out of order and the list has been completely sorted.

**Table 3-1**

BubbleSort first pass

| STEP | BEFORE | AFTER | COMMENTS |
|------|--------|-------|----------|
| 1 | **20, 30**, 10, 40 | **20, 30**, 10, 40 | The algorithm compares the first two elements (20 and 30); because they are in the correct order, no swap is needed. |
| 2 | 20, **30, 10**, 40 | 20, **10, 30**, 40 | The algorithm compares the next two elements (30 and 10); because they are out of order, the elements are swapped. |
| 3 | 20, 10, **30, 40** | 20, 10, **30, 40** | The algorithm compares the next two elements (30 and 40); because they are in the correct order, no swap is needed. |

As shown in Table 3-1, at the end of first pass, BubbleSort has performed one swap, and there is the possibility that the items are not yet completely sorted. Therefore, BubbleSort gives the list another pass, as depicted in Table 3-2.

**Table 3-2**

BubbleSort second pass

| STEP | BEFORE | AFTER | COMMENTS |
|------|--------|-------|----------|
| 1 | **20, 10**, 30, 40 | **10, 20**, 30, 40 | The algorithm compares the first two elements (20 and 10); because they are out of order, the elements are swapped. |
| 2 | 10, **20, 30**, 40 | 10, **20, 30**, 40 | The algorithm compares the next two elements (20 and 30); because they are in the correct order, no swap is needed. |
| 3 | 10, 20, **30, 40** | 10, 20, **30, 40** | The algorithm compares the next two elements (30 and 40); because they are in the correct order, no swap is needed. |

At the end of second pass, BubbleSort has performed one more swap, so it can't yet guarantee that the list is completely sorted. Thus, BubbleSort gives the list another pass, as shown in Table 3-3.

**Table 3-3**

BubbleSort third pass

When using BubbleSort, you can be assured that an array will be sorted in one less pass than the number of items. So, if there are four items (as in the example scenario), the array will be sorted (no matter what order it starts in) in three passes.

| Step | Before | After | Comments |
|---|---|---|---|
| 1 | **10, 20**, 30, 40 | **10, 20**, 30, 40 | The algorithm compares the first two elements (10 and 20); because they are in the correct order, no swap is needed. |
| 2 | 10, **20, 30**, 40 | 10, **20, 30**, 40 | The algorithm compares the next two elements (20 and 30); because they are in the correct order, no swap is needed. |
| 3 | 10, 20, **30, 40** | 10, 20, **30, 40** | The algorithm compares the next two elements (30 and 40); because they are in the correct order, no swap is needed. |

At the end of the third pass, BubbleSort didn't perform any swaps. This guarantees that the list is now in sorted order and the algorithm can finish.

In C#, the BubbleSort algorithm can be expressed by the following method:

```csharp
static int[] BubbleSort(int[] numbers)
{
    bool swapped;
    do
    {
        swapped = false;
        for (int i = 0; i < numbers.Length − 1; i++)
        {
            if (numbers[i] > numbers[i + 1])
            {
                //swap
                int temp = numbers[i + 1];
                numbers[i + 1] = numbers[i];
                numbers[i] = temp;
                swapped = true;
            }
        }
    } while (swapped == true);
    return numbers;
}
```

## Understanding QuickSort

The *QuickSort* algorithm uses the partitioning and comparison operations to arrange the elements of a list in the correct order.

The QuickSort algorithm uses the divide-and-conquer technique to continually partition a list until the size of the problem is small and hardly requires any sorting. The following steps explain this process in greater detail:

- A list of size zero or one is always sorted by itself.
- For a bigger list, pick any element in the list as a pivot element. Then, partition the list in such a way that all elements smaller than or equal to the pivot element go into the left list and all elements bigger than the pivot element go into the right list. Now, the combination of the left list, pivot element, and right list is always in sorted order if the left and the right list are in sorted order.
- The problem is now partitioned into two smaller lists, the left list and the right list.
- Both these lists are solved using the technique described in the bullets above.
- Finally, all the small sorted lists are merged in order to create the final complete sorted list.

The following table explains the QuickSort algorithm with a brief example.

**Table 3-4**

Visualizing QuickSort

| STEP | DATA TO BE SORTED | COMMENTS |
|---|---|---|
| 1 | 50, 10, **30**, 20, 40 | Start with an unsorted list and pick a pivot element—in this case 30. |
| 2 | 20, **10** 30 50, **40** | Partition the list, with items less than the pivot going to the left list and items greater than the pivot going to the right list. Then, to sort the left list, pick a pivot (here, 10). Similarly, to sort the right list, pick a pivot (here, 40) for that list. |
| 3 | - 10 20 30 - 40 50 | In the left list, 20 is greater than 10, and in the right list, 50 is greater than 40; therefore, both 20 and 50 go into the right list. This yields lists of only one number, which are all by definition sorted. |
| 4 | 10, 20, 30, 40, 50 | All the small sorted lists are merged to create the final complete sorted list. |

So far, the main shortcoming of the QuickSort algorithm might appear to be the additional memory required by the creation of separate smaller lists. However, creating separate lists is not necessary. Using a slightly modified technique, the array can be partitioned in place, as shown in the following code listing:

```
static int Partition (int[] numbers, int left,
       int right, int pivotIndex)
```

```
{
        int pivotValue = numbers[pivotIndex];
    // move pivot element to the end
    int temp = numbers[right];
    numbers[right] = numbers[pivotIndex];
    numbers[pivotIndex] = temp;

    // newPivot stores the index of the first
    // number bigger than pivot
    int newPivot = left;
    for (int i = left; i < right; i++)
    {
        if (numbers[i] <= pivotValue)
        {
        temp = numbers[newPivot];
        numbers[newPivot] = numbers[i];
        numbers[i] = temp;
        newPivot++;
        }
    }

    //move pivot element to its sorted position
    temp = numbers[right];
    numbers[right] = numbers[newPivot];
    numbers[newPivot] = temp;

    return newPivot;

}
```

With this technique, first the pivot element is moved to the end of the array. Then, all the elements less than or equal to the pivot element are moved to the front of the array. Finally, the pivot element is placed just before the element greater than itself, effectively partitioning the array.

This partitioning algorithm can then be used by QuickSort to partition the list, reduce the problem to smaller problems, and recursively solve it:

```
static int[] QuickSort(int[] numbers,
     int left, int right)
{
    if (right > left)
    {
        int pivotIndex = left + (right - left) / 2;
        //partition the array
        pivotIndex = Partition(
            numbers, left, right, pivotIndex);
        //sort the left partition
        QuickSort(
```

```
            numbers, left, pivotIndex − 1);
        // sort the right partition
        QuickSort(
            numbers, pivotIndex + 1, right);
    }
    return numbers;
}
```

**CERTIFICATION READY**
Do you understand
common sorting
algorithms?
3.3

Because of its partitioning approach, the QuickSort algorithm is much faster than the BubbleSort algorithm.

## SKILL SUMMARY

**IN THIS LESSON, YOU LEARNED THE FOLLOWING:**

- Application lifecycle management (ALM) refers to the various activities that revolve around a new software product from its inception to the time when it matures and perhaps retires.
- Software testing is the process of verifying software against its requirements. Testing takes place after most developmental work is complete.
- Data structures are techniques for organizing and storing data in computer memory. How the data is stored affects how it is retrieved and manipulated. Understanding a data structure involves understanding not only the storage pattern, but also the methods used to create, access, and manipulate the structure.
- An array is a collection of items of the same data type that are stored in a contiguous memory location and addressed using one or more indices.
- A queue is a collection of items in which the first item added to the collection is the first one to be removed.
- A stack is a collection of items in which the last item added to the collection is the first one to be removed.
- A linked list is a collection of nodes arranged in such a way that each node contains a link to the next node in the sequence.
- The BubbleSort algorithm uses a series of comparison and swap operations to arrange the elements of a list in the correct order.
- The QuickSort algorithm uses partitioning and comparison operations to arrange the elements of a list in the correct order.

## ■ Knowledge Assessment

### Fill in the Blank

*Complete the following sentences by writing the correct word or words in the blanks provided.*

1. In _____ testing, testers use their knowledge of system internals to assess the system.

2. Usually, with every new fix, software testers run a battery of _____ to make sure that all functionality that was known to be working is still working.

3. The BubbleSort algorithm uses a series of _____ and _____ operations to arrange the elements of a list in the correct order.

4. A(n) _____ is a collection of items in which the last item added to the collection is the first one to be removed.

5. _____ is the process of determining the detailed business requirements for a new software system.

6. A linked list is a collection of nodes such that each node contains a(n) _____ to the next node in the sequence.

7. The _____ operation adds an item to a queue, whereas the _____ operation removes an item from a queue.

8. The QuickSort algorithm uses _____ and comparison operations to arrange the elements of a list in the correct order.

9. A(n) _____ is responsible for analyzing business needs and converting them into requirements that can be executed by the development team.

10. Alpha testing and beta testing both are part of the _____ testing of a system.

## Multiple Choice

*Circle the letter that corresponds to the best answer.*

1. The product that you are developing is not yet finished, but you would like to release the product to a wider customer audience for feedback and testing. Under which of the following testing levels would this activity fall?
   a. Integration testing
   b. System testing
   c. Acceptance testing
   d. Regression testing

2. The testers of a software application have access to its source code, and they plan to write test cases that ensure that the methods return correct values. Which of the following testing levels will this activity fall under?
   a. Integration testing
   b. Unit testing
   c. Alpha testing
   d. Beta testing

3. Which of the following data structures allows direct access to all of its items?
   a. Array
   b. Stack
   c. Queue
   d. Linked list

4. Which of the following activities in the application lifecycle is used by an architect to create the technical blueprint of a system?
   a. Requirements analysis
   b. Design
   c. Development
   d. Maintenance

5. In your application, you are using a queue data structure to manipulate information. You need to find which data item will be processed next, but you don't want to actually process that data item yet. Which of the following queue operations will you use?
   a. Enqueue
   b. Dequeue
   c. Peek
   d. Contains

6. You are developing a program that requires you to track the method calls. You can only invoke one method at a time. However, a method call may in turn invoke other methods. When a method ends, it returns control back to the calling method. Which data structure should you use to keep track of these method calls?
   a. Queue
   b. Array
   c. Linked list
   d. Stack

7. You are developing a program that simulates a job processor. Often, the jobs come faster than you can process them, and in such cases, the jobs wait for their turn to be processed. You need to make sure that the job that arrived first is the first to be processed as well. Which of the following data structures is best suited for this requirement?
   a. Array
   b. Queue
   c. Linked list
   d. Stack

8. You write the following code in a program:

   ```
   int[] numbers = {2, 3, 1, 4};

   numbers [2] = 4;
   ```

   What will be the contents of the array after the second statement is executed?
   a. {2, 4, 1, 4}
   b. {2, 3, 4, 4}
   c. {2, 4, 1, 2}
   d. {4, 3, 1, 4}

9. You are developing a program that performs frequent insert and delete operations on the data. Your requirement also dictates the capability to access previous and next records when the user presses the previous or next button. Which of the following data structures will best suit your requirements?
   a. Array
   b. Circular linked list
   c. Linked list
   d. Doubly linked list

10. You are developing a program that performs frequent insert and delete operations on the data. The data items need to be accessed like a stack with last-in, first-out functionality. Your solution must require as little memory as possible. Which of the following data structures will best suit these requirements?
    a. Array
    b. Circular linked list
    c. Linked list
    d. Doubly linked list

# ■ Competency Assessment

## Scenario 3-1: Using Arrays

You are writing a program that uses a two-dimensional array. The array has four rows and five columns. You need to print the largest element in each row of the array. How would you write such a program?

### Scenario 3-2: Using Queues

You are writing a program that uses two queues. The data in each queue is already in ascending order. You need to process the contents of both queues in such a way that the output is printed on the screen in sorted order. How would you write such a program?

## ■ Proficiency Assessment

### Scenario 3-3: Using Stacks

You are writing a program that uses two stacks. The data in each stack is already in descending order. You need to process the contents of both stacks in such a way that the output is printed on the screen in ascending order. How would you write such a program?

### Scenario 3-4: Using Linked Lists

You are writing a program that stores a list of product names in a linked list. The user will enter a product name, and your program needs to check whether the linked list contains the given product. How would you write such a program?

# Understanding Web Applications

## LESSON SKILL MATRIX

| SKILLS/CONCEPTS | MTA EXAM OBJECTIVE | MTA EXAM OBJECTIVE NUMBER |
|---|---|---|
| Understanding Web Page Development | Understand Web page development. | 4.1 |
| Understanding ASP.NET Application Development | Understand Microsoft ASP.NET Web application development. | 4.2 |
| Understanding IIS Web Hosting | Understand Web hosting. | 4.3 |
| Understanding Web Services Development | Understand Web services. | 4.4 |

## KEY TERMS

cascading style sheets (CSS)

client-side programming

client-side state management

Hypertext Markup Language (HTML)

Internet Information Services (IIS)

JavaScript

Simple Object Access Protocol (SOAP)

server-side programming

server-side state management

state management

virtual directory

Web hosting

Web services

Web service description language (WSDL)

Web site

You are a software developer for a large business organization. You need to develop an application that can be used over a network such as the World Wide Web. The application will be deployed on a Windows Web server, but the application's users will use multiple operating systems and Web browsers.

## ■ Understanding Web Page Development

**THE BOTTOM LINE**
A Web page is a document that is served over the World Wide Web (WWW) and can be displayed by a Web browser. Web pages are developed using the Hypertext Markup Language (HTML) and are stored on a Web server. Web browsers download the requested HTML from the Web server and render it on the user's screen.

85

The World Wide Web (also known as WWW or "the Web") is a system of interconnected hypertext documents and other resources (such as images and video) that can be accessed via the Internet. Multiple technologies work together to make the WWW possible. In this section, we will discuss two of these technologies:

- Hypertext Transfer Protocol (HTTP)
- *Hypertext Markup Language (HTML)*

HTTP is the underlying communication protocol used by the World Wide Web. HTTP provides the common language that Web servers and Web browsers use in order to communicate.

HTTP uses a Uniform Resource Locator (URL) to uniquely identify and address each resource on the Internet. A URL is essentially a Web address and looks like this: http://www.microsoft .com/en/us/default.aspx. Each URL starts with a protocol. In this example, the protocol is HTTP. You may also notice the HTTPS (secure HTTP) protocol in use for secure applications in which data needs to be encrypted before it is transmitted over the network. After the protocol, the next part of a URL is the address of the Web server (here, www.microsoft.com), followed by the location of the resource within the Web server (/en/us/), and finally, the requested resource itself (default.aspx). All documents, images, videos, and other resources on the Web are identified by a URL.

When a browser sends an HTTP request for a Web page to a Web server (both the Web page and the server are identified by a URL), the server prepares an HTTP response for the browser. This response specifies the content and layout of the Web page.

**TAKE NOTE** * The terms "Internet" and "the Web" are often used interchangeably, but they are actually distinct and should not be confused. The Internet is a global data communications system that provides connectivity among computers. In contrast, the Web is one of several services available on the Internet that allows users to access hyperlinked resources.

The language that the Web server and Web browser use to describe a Web page is Hypertext Markup Language (HTML). HTML is a text-based language that uses various markup tags that describe how content is displayed. HTML allows images, videos, and other objects to be referenced in a file to create multimedia Web pages. HTML can also embed scripts (such as JavaScript) that affect the behavior of Web pages, and it can be used to include cascading style sheets (CSS) to define the formatting and layout of a page's content. The Web browser reads the HTML code and renders the results on the screen.

A Web page may contain hyperlinks to other resources, such as images and videos. Each of these resources is identified by its own URL. Thus, in order to render a page completely, the browser will make additional HTTP requests to get these resources and display them as part of the Web page.

In the following sections, you'll learn more about the various components that make up a Web page, including HTML, CSS, and JavaScript.

## Understanding HTML

Hypertext Markup Language (HTML) is the language used by Web servers and browsers to describe a Web page.

The purpose of HTML is to provide a standard language for describing Web pages so that different Web browsers can understand this language and display the corresponding page. HTML is a text-based language, which means that you can write and edit HTML pages using any text editor. When HTML is sent to a Web browser, the complete text of the page is sent. In fact, most browsers allow you to view the HTML source code for a Web page.

HTML consists of a set of tags (also called as HTML elements) that define the structure and content of a page. For example, the <html> tag specifies the beginning of an HTML document. HTML tags are always surrounded by angle brackets and always used in pairs. In particular, each starting tag has a matching ending tag. Ending tags contain a forward slash to indicate that they are such. For example, the ending tag for <html> is </html>.

An HTML page has two distinct parts: a header and a body. The header is enclosed within the <head> and </head> tags and is used to provide a document title and links to external items that may be used in the page, such as CSS files and JavaScript files. The body is enclosed within the <body> and </body> tags, and it is used to provide the complete structure and content of the page that will be displayed within a Web browser.

Here is an example of an HTML tag that displays an image:

```
<img height="400px" width="400px"
alt="Mimas Cassini" src=
"http://upload.wikimedia.org/wikipedia/commons/b/bc/Mimas_Cassini.jpg"/>
```

Notice that the <img> tag specifies additional attributes. For example, the src attribute specifies the location of the image file, and the height and the width attributes specify what dimensions to use when rendering the image in a browser.

Now, consider another example of an HTML tag:

```
<a href="http://en.wikipedia.org/wiki/Mimas_(moon)">
Saturn's moon</a>
```

Here, <a> is the anchor tag, which is used to create hyperlinks on a Web page. The href attribute associated with this tag specifies the target URL, and the text within the anchor tag is that which is displayed as a link.

The following exercise demonstrates the steps involved in creating an HTML document.

 **WORK WITH HTML**

**GET READY.** To create an HTML document, perform these actions:

1. Open Visual Studio. Create a new project based on the ASP.NET Empty Web Application template. Name the project WorkingWithHTML and name the solution Lesson04.

2. Select **Project > Add New Item**, then select the **HTML Page** template. Name the file default.htm.

3. Replace the default code in the HTML file with the following:

```
<html xmlns="http://www.w3.org/1999/xhtml">
<head>
    <title>Saturn's Moon</title>
</head>
```

```
<body>
<h1>Mimas Cassini</h1>
The img tag is used to display the picture of a
<a href="http://en.wikipedia.org/wiki/Mimas_(moon)">
    Saturn's moon</a>: <br />
<img height="400px" width="400px"
    alt="Mimas Cassini"
    src="http://goo.gl/3BeK"/>
</body>
</html>
```

4. Select **Debug > Start Debugging** (or press **F5**). The default.htm page will open in a Web browser. The output should look similar to Figure 4-1, where you can see the <img> and <a> tags in action.

**Figure 4-1**

A simple HTML page that contains an image and hyperlink

## Understanding Cascading Style Sheets

*Cascading style sheets (CSS)* enable you to store a Web page's style and formatting information separate from the HTML code. This separation makes it easier to update the look and feel of your Web site. Visual Studio includes tools to build and preview your style sheets.

CSS is a language that describes information about displaying a Web page. When rendering Web pages in a browser, HTML specifies what will be displayed, and the cascading style sheets (CSS) specify how that material will be displayed. For example, HTML can specify that your document has a H1 heading with a given text, and CSS can specify the font and color that will be applied to that heading.

CSS enables you to separate the layout of a Web page from its content. This separation allows you to change one without affecting the other. Mixing content and style together reduces the maintainability of a Web site. For example, say you want to change the color and font of all H1 headings on your Web site. One approach may be to open an HTML editor and modify each file on the Web site that uses the H1 tag. This might be an acceptable solution if the Web site has just one or two pages, but what if the site has a large number of pages—for example, 50 or 100? Imagine manually changing each page! If such changes are requested often, the Web development process will be boring and error prone. After all, how can you ensure that you did not miss any H1 tags?

Fortunately, with CSS, you can put all such styling information in a separate file and connect that file to all pages on a Web site. Then, once the CSS file is set up, you can modify any style (such as the color and font of H1 headings) simply by changing the style in the CSS file—and this single change will affect all pages on the Web site.

## DESIGNING CASCADING STYLE SHEETS

The CSS language is text-based and easy to read and understand. The following is an example of an HTML page that defines CSS styles:

```
<html xmlns="http://www.w3.org/1999/xhtml">
<head runat="server">
    <title>Understanding CSS</title>
    <style type="text/css">
        body
        {
            font-family: Verdana;
            font-size: 9pt;
        }
        div
        {
            color:Red;
        }
        .block
        {
            background-color: Yellow;
            border-color: Blue;
            border-width: thin;
            border-style: outset;
            font-family: Arial;
        }
    </style>
</head>
<body>
    Sample body text <br />
    <div>Sample DIV text</div>
    <div class="block">Sample DIV text
        with block class</div>
    <span class="block">Sample SPAN text
        with block class</span>
</body>
</html>
```

Note that the CSS definitions must be inside the <style> element and are defined under the <head> element. This particular CSS defines two element styles and a class style. The first style applies to the HTML body element and specifies that all text in the body element should use the Verdana font with 9-point font size. The second element style specifies that the text within the DIV element should be written in red. Finally, a class named "block" is defined. CSS class definitions are prefixed with a dot ("."). The contents of any HTML element that uses this class will be displayed with yellow background and a border. When you display this particular page in a browser, it should appear as shown in Figure 4-2.

**Figure 4-2**

Formatting HTML with cascading style sheets

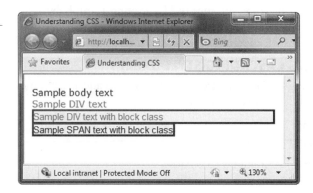

In the figure, notice that the highlighted text is displayed as a result of the block class. However, the block CSS class does not specify the color of the text. In the first line of highlighted text, the block class is applied to the DIV element; in the second line of highlighted text, the block class is applied to the SPAN element. In the first case, because the block class is applied to a DIV text, the color style of the DIV element is carried over in the final rendering.

In the previous example, the CSS file was written inside the HTML file. A more useful approach is to write the CSS in its own separate file and then link the HTML file to this CSS file. You will learn how to do so in the following exercise.

## WORK WITH CSS FILES

**GET READY.** To write a CSS file and link it to an HTML file, perform these steps:

1. Add a new project based on the ASP.NET Empty Web Application template to the Lesson04 solution. Name the project UnderstandingCSS.

2. Select **Project > Add New Item**. Select the **Style Sheet** template. Name the file styles.css. Replace the default code in the file with the following:

```
body
{
    font-family: Verdana;
    font-size: 9pt;
}
div
{
    color:Red;
}
```

```
.block

{

        background-color: Yellow;

        border-color: Blue;

        border-width: thin;

        border-style: outset;

        font-family: Arial;

}
```

3. Select **Project > Add New Item**, then select the **HTML Page** template. Name the file default.htm. Replace the default code in the file with the following:

```
<!DOCTYPE html PUBLIC

"–//W3C//DTD XHTML 1.0 Transitional//EN"

"http://www.w3.org/TR/xhtml1/DTD/xhtml1–
        transitional.dtd">

<html xmlns="http://www.w3.org/1999/xhtml">

<head>

        <link rel="STYLESHEET"

                type="text/css" href="styles.css" />

        <title>Understanding CSS</title>

</head>

<body>

        Sample body text <br />

        <div>Sample DIV text</div>

        <div class="block">Sample DIV text

                with block class</div>

        <span class="block">Sample SPAN text

                with block class</span>

</body>

</html>
```

4. Select **Debug > Start Debugging** (or press **F5**). The default.htm page will open in a Web browser, and the output should be similar to Figure 4-2 (presented earlier).

When CSS are stored in separate files, the user's browser will download and store these files locally. Therefore, they can be used on multiple pages without any need to download them again. This reduces unnecessary data transfer.

As shown in the example exercise, the HTML <link> element is used to link a CSS file with an HTML page:

```
<link rel="STYLESHEET"

    type="text/css" href="styles.css" />
```

The <link> element is always put within the <head> element, and the href attribute specifies the address of the CSS file to use. To link multiple pages with the same CSS file, you'll need to put the <link> element within each HTML page.

Visual Studio includes a built-in style designer that can help you design new CSS styles or modify existing styles. When you open a .css file, you'll see a new menu named Styles. From this menu, you can create a new style by selecting Styles > Add Style Rule. You can also modify the currently selected style by selecting the Styles > Build Style option. This option opens the Modify Style dialog box, as shown in Figure 4-3.

**Figure 4-3**

The Modify Style dialog box

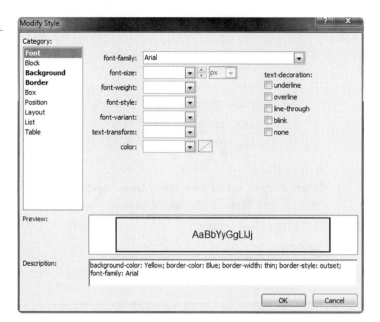

## Understanding JavaScript

*JavaScript* is a client-side scripting language that runs inside Web browsers to help create far more interactive Web pages than are possible with only HTML. JavaScript is used in millions of Web pages and is supported by all modern Web browsers.

JavaScript is used to make Web sites more responsive and Web pages more interactive. JavaScript accomplishes this by executing the code on the client side (the Web browser) and by minimizing unnecessary round-trips to and from the Web server. Let's take an example in which a user needs to enter personal details on a Web page, such as name, email address, and phone number. A common requirement is to perform data validation to ensure that the input fields are not empty and the user's email address and phone number have been provided in the required form. Without JavaScript, you would need to submit the form to the server, which will perform data validation and return the results to the client. This transmission of information takes time and degrades the user experience. However, a JavaScript solution can perform this type of data validation from within the browser, providing a better user experience.

As previously mentioned, JavaScript code executes locally within the Web browser (the client), as opposed to on the Web server. Therefore, JavaScript is sometimes also called a client-side scripting language, and programming with JavaScript is referred to as client-side programming.

The runtime behavior of client-side code execution depends on the browser that executes it. However, this behavior is independent of server technology or programming framework. Thus, for JavaScript that is being executed in a Web browser, it does not matter whether the Web page was generated by ASP.NET or PHP or whether the page is being served by a Windows Web server or a Linux Web server.

JavaScript and the C# programming language both use a syntax influenced by the C programming language. Still, JavaScript and C# are very different in how they are executed. In particular, JavaScript is executed by the Web browser, and JavaScript code is interpreted rather than compiled, as in the case of C#.

**TAKE NOTE***

Many modern Web sites provide a highly interactive experience rivaling that of desktop applications. Such sites can be developed using Ajax programming. Ajax is shorthand for "Asynchronous JavaScript and XML." Ajax uses JavaScript extensively in order to provide responsive Web applications. The ASP.NET AJAX framework lets you implement Ajax functionality on ASP.NET Web pages.

All JavaScript code must be placed inside the <script> element. The <script> element is usually placed inside the <head> element, although this is not required. Multiple <script> elements may exist within a single page. To see JavaScript in action, try the following exercise.

### ➔ WORK WITH JAVASCRIPT

**GET READY.** To begin working with JavaScript, perform the following tasks:

1. Add a new project based on the ASP.NET Empty Web Application template to the Lesson04 solution. Name the project UnderstandingJavaScript.

2. Select **Project > Add New Item**, then select the **HTML Page** template. Name the file default.htm. Replace the default code in the file with the following:

```
<!DOCTYPE html PUBLIC
"-//W3C//DTD XHTML 1.0 Transitional//EN"
"http://www.w3.org/TR/xhtml1/DTD/xhtml1-
    transitional.dtd">
<html xmlns="http://www.w3.org/1999/xhtml">
<head>
    <title>Understanding JavaScript</title>
    <script type="text/javascript"
        language="javascript">
        username = prompt("Please enter your name");

        message = "Hello, " + username +
          ". Your name has ";
        nameLen = username.length;
        if (nameLen > 5)
            message = message + "more than ";
        else if (nameLen < 5)
            message = message + "less than ";
        else
            message = message + "exactly ";
        message = message + "5 characters.";

        alert(message);
    </script>
</head>
<body>
</body>
</html>
```

3. Select **Debug > Start Debugging** (or press **F5**). The default.htm page will open in a Web browser. Notice that the JavaScript code prompts you to enter your name. Once you have done so, a dialog box displays a message based on the length of your name, as shown in Figures 4-4 and 4-5.

**Figure 4-4**

JavaScript user prompt

**Figure 4-5**

JavaScript dialog box

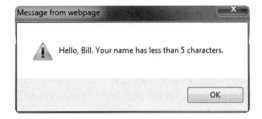

As with CSS files, you can also put your JavaScript code in a separate file and link this file with an HTML file by using the script element, as shown below:

```
<script src="SampleScript.js">
</script>
```

Here, the SampleScript.js file contains all the JavaScript code, and the script element links to this file by using the src attribute. Storing JavaScript in external files offers many advantages:

- **Improved maintainability:** If you use the same JavaScript code on each page of a Web site, you can store the code on a central page rather than repeating it on every page. This way, when it's time to modify the JavaScript code, you'll have to change the code in only one place.
- **Improved performance:** Storing JavaScript code in a separate file reduces the size of a Web page. Also, browsers can download and cache the external JavaScript file so that it is not downloaded again unless it is modified.

Visual Studio includes full IntelliSense support for JavaScript code. Even ASP.NET controls, like the TreeView control or the validation controls, use JavaScript where possible to render content dynamically.

## Understanding Client-Side vs. Server-Side Programming

Whether a program is *client-side* or *server-side* depends on where the program is ultimately executed.

***Client-side programming*** refers to programs that execute completely on a user's local computer. Examples of client-side programs include the Windows Forms application and JavaScript code that executes within a Web browser. Client-side programs do not consume server resources.

On the other hand, ***server-side programming*** refers to programs that are executed completely on a server and make use of the server's computational resources. Here, the only client resources that are used are those involved in actually retrieving the processing results from the server. Web applications and Web services are examples of server-side programming. This type of programming uses a server-side technology such as ASP.NET, PHP, or Ruby on Rails.

Recently, hybrid applications that use both client- and server-side programming have become increasingly popular. For instance, you can design smart-client applications that run locally on client computers but make use of Web services to accomplish certain tasks. In fact, Ajax applications use a mix of server-side programming and client-side code to create interactive and highly responsive Web applications.

ASP.NET allows you to create applications that completely execute on the server or hybrid Ajax applications that provide fast, responsive interfaces while storing most of their data on the Web.

**CERTIFICATION READY**
Do you understand how to use HTML, JavaScript, and CSS for Web page development?
4.1

## Understanding ASP.NET Application Development

**THE BOTTOM LINE** ASP.NET is the part of the .NET Framework that enables you to develop programmable Web forms and Web services. As with any .NET Framework application, you can develop ASP.NET applications in any language that is compatible with the .NET common language runtime, including Visual Basic and C#.

The ASP.NET infrastructure has two main parts:

- A set of classes and interfaces that enables communication between the Web browser and Web server. These classes are organized in the System.Web namespace.
- A runtime process, also known as the ASP.NET worker process (aspnet_wp.exe), that handles the Web request for ASP.NET resources.

At a higher level, an ASP.NET Web application is executed through a series of HTTP requests and response messages between the client browser and the Web server. This process occurs as follows:

1. The user requests a resource from a Web server by typing a URL in the Web browser. The browser sends an HTTP request to the destination Web server.
2. The Web server analyzes the HTTP request and searches for a process capable of executing the request.
3. The result of the HTTP request is returned to the client browser in the form of an HTTP response.
4. The browser reads the HTTP response and renders it as a Web page to the user.

This process is represented in Figure 4-6.

**Figure 4-6**

Communication between a client and a Web server

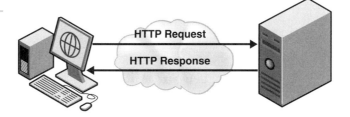

As a developer, you should know what happens behind the scenes when a Web server executes a request for an ASP.NET page. The following steps describe this process:

1. When the Internet Information Service (IIS) receives an HTTP request, it uses the file-name extension to determine which Internet Server Application Programming Interface (ISAPI) program to run to process the request. When the request is for an ASP.NET page, it passes the request to the ISAPI DLL capable of handling requests for ASP.NET pages, which is aspnet_isapi.dll.

2. The aspnet_isapi.dll process passes the request to the ASP.NET worker process (aspnet_wp.exe), which fulfills the request.

3. The ASP.NET worker process compiles the .aspx file into an assembly and instructs the Common Language Runtime (CLR) to execute the assembly.

4. When the assembly executes, it takes the services of various classes in the .NET Framework class library to accomplish its work and generate response messages for the requesting client.

5. The ASP.NET worker process collects the responses generated by the execution of the Web page, creates a response packet, and passes it to the aspnet_isapi.dll process.

6. Aspnet_isapi.dll forwards the response packet to IIS, which in turn passes the response to the requesting client machine.

Prior to execution, each ASP.NET page is converted into a class. This class derives most of its functionality from the System.Web.UI.Page class. The Page class provides several important properties, such as Request, Response, Session, and Server.

**TAKE NOTE** *

The Page class provides several important methods and properties that control how a page request is processed. For the complete list of methods and properties, visit http://msdn. microsoft.com/en-us/library/system.web.ui.page.aspx.

## Understanding ASP.NET Page Life Cycle and Event Model

During its execution, an ASP.NET page passes through many distinct stages of processing. Each of these stages itself goes through specific processing steps, such as initialization, loading, running event-handler code, and rendering.

As a page executes, it goes through various stages of processing. The page also fires a few events to which you can attach an event handler in order to execute custom code at different stages of page processing. In fact, ASP.NET developers must have a good understanding of the page life cycle so that they can write code that is executed at exactly the desired stage of page processing.

Table 4.1 lists the different life cycle stages and their associated events.

**TAKE NOTE** *

In a typical contact form, you enter information and press a submit button. When you submit this page, the page can process the submitted data to take some action, such as storing the information in a database or sending an email. In many cases, the initial page is displayed again with a confirmation of the form submission. A *postback* occurs when the information is posted to the same Web page for processing. A postback is different from the initial load of the page because the page receives additional information (such as form data) as part of the postback.

**Table 4-1**

Important stages in the ASP.NET page life cycle

| STAGE | MEANING | ASSOCIATED EVENTS |
|---|---|---|
| Page request | When a request for a page is received, the page life cycle begins. At this point, ASP.NET decides whether the page can be readily served from the cache or whether it needs to be parsed and compiled. | |
| Start | The start stage involves determining whether the request is a postback or a new request. Several page properties, such as Request, Response, IsPostBack, and UICulture, are set at this stage. | PreInit |
| Initialization | During the initialization stage, all the controls on the page are initialized and made available. An event handler for the Init event is the best place for code that you want to be executed prior to further page processing. | Init |
| Load | If the request is a postback, the load stage is used to restore control properties with information from view state and control state. A method that handles the Load event is the best place to store initialization code for any controls specific to this page. | Load |
| Postback event handling | If the request is a postback, the control event handlers are called during this stage. Then, the input values are validated and the IsValid property for the Page class is set. | |
| Prerendering | This stage signals that the page is just about to render its contents. An event handler for the PreRender event is the last chance to modify the page's output before it is sent to the client. | PreRender |
| Rendering | At this stage, the page calls the Render method for each control and populates the response that will be sent to the Web browser. | |
| Unload | During the unload stage, the response is sent to the client and page cleanup is performed. As part of this cleanup, page properties such as Request and Response are discarded. | Unload |

When you want to handle an event, you must write code that registers a method to handle the event (also called as event handler) with the event. This is usually done using the common event registration pattern employed throughout the .NET Framework:

*object.event* += new EventHandler(*eventhandler*);

Here, replace *object* with the name of the object that exposes the event, *event* with the name of the event, and *eventhandler* with the name of the method that handles the event.

Note, however, that ASP.NET provides six special methods that are recognized as event handlers by default and do not need the above registration code. These are the specially named methods Page_Init, Page_Load, Page_DataBind, Page_PreRender, and Page_Unload. These methods are treated as event handlers for the corresponding events exposed by the Page class. This automatic event wiring is controlled by the AutoEventWireup attribute of the @Page directive. By default, the value of this attribute is true, meaning that these specially named methods are automatically wired up with their corresponding events.

**UNDERSTAND THE ASP.NET PAGE LIFE CYCLE**

**GET READY.** To see how different events of the Page class are executed, perform the following actions:

1. Create a new project based on the ASP.NET Empty Web Application template to the Lesson04 solution. Name the project PageEvents.

2. Select **Project > Add New Item**. Select the **Web Form** template. Name the file WebForm1.aspx.

3. In the HTML markup for the page (WebForm1.aspx), make sure that the AutoEventWireup attribute for the @Page directive is set to true:

    ```
    <%@ Page Language="C#" AutoEventWireup="true"
    CodeBehind="WebForm1.aspx.cs"
    Inherits="PageEvents.WebForm1" %>
    ```

4. Right-click in the code window and select **View Code** from the shortcut menu to switch to the code view. Replace the code in the code-behind file (WebForm1.aspx.cs) with the following:

```csharp
using System;
namespace PageEvents
{
    public partial class WebForm1
        : System.Web.UI.Page
    {
        protected void Page_Load
            (object sender, EventArgs e)
        {
            Response.Write
                ("Message from Page_Load. <br/>");
        }
        protected void Page_Init
            (object sender, EventArgs e)
        {
            Response.Write
                ("Message from Page_Init. <br/>");
        }
        protected void Page_PreRender
            (object sender, EventArgs e)
        {
            Response.Write
                ("Message from Page_PreRender. <br/>");
        }
        protected void Page_PreInit
            (object sender, EventArgs e)
        {
            Response.Write
                ("Message from Page_PreInit. <br/>");
        }
    }
}
```

5. Select **Debug > Start Debugging** (or press **F5**). The default.htm page will open in a Web browser, as shown in Figure 4-7.

**Figure 4-7**

Web form displaying the order of event execution for an ASP.NET page

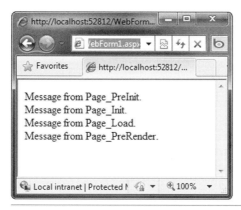

**Figure 4-7**

Web form displaying the order of event execution for an ASP.NET page

In the example exercise, note that the characters <% and %> are used to embed code blocks in the HTML markup of a page. The code inside these embedded blocks is executed during the page's rendering stage. Within the embedded code blocks, the syntax <%=*expression*> is used to resolve an expression and return its value into the block. For example, consider the following block of code:

```
<i><% = DateTime.Now.ToShortDateString() %></i>
```

When executed, this code will display the current date in italicized format:

*12/01/2010*

The @Page directive specifies various attributes that control how ASP.NET will render a page. For example, in this exercise, attributes of the @Page directive specify the following:

- C# is the programming language for this Web page (Language="C#")
- The page's events are auto-wired (AutoEventWireup=true)
- The name of the code file that contains the class associated with the page (CodeBehind="WebForm1.aspx.cs")
- The class name for the page to inherit (Inherits="PageEvents.WebForm1")

## Understanding State Management

> State management is an important issue for Web applications because of the disconnected nature of HTTP. There are both client-side and server-side techniques available for state management.

*State management* is the process of maintaining state for a Web page across round-trips. The values of the variables and controls collectively make up the state of a Web page.

ASP.NET provides several techniques for preserving state information across page postbacks. These techniques can be broadly categorized as either client-side or server-side, depending on where the resources are consumed.

## INTRODUCING CLIENT-SIDE STATE MANAGEMENT

*Client-side state management* use HTML code and the capabilities of the Web browser to store state information on the client computer. The following techniques are used for storing state information on the client side:

- **Query strings:** Here, state is maintained by putting the data as a set of key-value pairs in the query string portion of a page URL. For example, the following URL embeds a query string key (q) and value (television) pair: http://www.bing.com/search?q=television. To retrieve the value of the key in an ASP.NET page, use the expression Request.QueryString["q"]. QueryString is a property of the Request object, and it gets the collection of all the query-string variables.

- **Cookies:** Cookies are small packets of information that are stored by a Web browser locally on the user's computer. Cookies are commonly employed to store user preferences and shopping cart contents and to give users a personalized browsing experience on subsequent visits to a Web page. The HttpCookie class represents a cookie in your code. The following code shows how to set a cookie on a client computer:

```
HttpCookie cookie =
    new HttpCookie("Name", "Bob");
cookie.Expires = DateTime.Now.AddMinutes(10);
Response.Cookies.Add(cookie);
```

Similarly, the following piece of code shows how to read a cookie:

```
if (Request.Cookies["Name"] != null)
{
    name = Request.Cookies["Name"].Value;
}
```

- **Hidden fields:** Hidden fields contain information that is not displayed on a Web page but is still part of the page's HTML code. Hidden fields can be created by using the <input type="hidden"> HTML element. The ASP.NET HTML Server control HtmlInputHidden also maps to this HTML element.

- **ViewState:** ViewState is the mechanism ASP.NET uses to maintain the state of controls across page postbacks. To facilitate this, when ASP.NET executes a page, it collects the values of all nonpostback controls that are modified in the code and formats them into a single encoded string. This string is stored in a hidden field in a control named __VIEWSTATE. By default, ViewState is enabled in an ASP.NET application. You can disable ViewState at the level of a control by setting the EnableViewState property of the control to false:

```
<asp:GridView ID="GridView1"
    runat="server" EnableViewState="false" />
```

In addition, you can disable ViewState at the page level by setting the EnableViewState attribute of the Page directive to false:

```
<%@ Page EnableViewState="false" %>
```

Finally, you can disable ViewState at the application level by adding the following line to the web.config file:

```
<pages enableViewState="false" />
```

## INTRODUCING SERVER-SIDE STATE MANAGEMENT

*Server-side state management* uses server resources to store state information. Using server-side techniques eliminates the possibility that a user will try to hack the client-side code or read the session data. However, storing and processing session information on a server increases the server's load and requires additional server resources to serve the Web pages.

ASP.NET supports server-side state management at two levels:

- **Session state:** An ASP.NET application creates a unique session for each user who sends a request to the application. ASP.NET distinctly identifies each of these sessions by sending a unique SessionId to the requesting URL. This SessionId is transmitted as a cookie or embedded in the URL, depending on the application's configuration. The ability to uniquely identify and relate requests can be used to store session-specific data that is also known as the session state of the Web application. A common example of session state is storing shopping cart contents for users as they browse through a Web-based store.

> **TAKE NOTE**\*
>
> The session state can be configured for storage on another server or a SQL server. This is useful when a user's request can be processed by one of the many servers in a Web farm. A Web farm is a collection of Web servers used collectively to serve a Web site. Web farms are necessary to support traffic on popular Web sites.

- **Application state:** Application state is used to store data that is used throughout an application. Application state can be easily accessed through the Application property of the Page class. This property provides access to the HttpApplicationState object that stores the application state as a collection of key-value pairs.

The following exercise shows how to use the session state. This exercise involves two Web forms. The WebForm1.aspx gets a user name and stores it in the session state. The form then transfers the user to the WebForm2.aspx, which retrieves the user name from the session.

 **USE SESSION STATE**

**GET READY.** To use session state, perform the following steps:

1. Add a new project based on the ASP.NET Empty Web Application template to the Lesson04 solution. Name the project UsingSessionState.
2. Select **Project > Add New Item**. Select the **Web Form** template. Name the file WebForm1.aspx
3. Change the HTML markup of the WebForm1.aspx to the following:

```
<%@ Page Language="C#" AutoEventWireup="true"
       CodeBehind="WebForm1.aspx.cs"
       Inherits="UsingSessionState.WebForm1" %>
<html xmlns="http://www.w3.org/1999/xhtml">
<head runat="server">
    <title></title>
</head>
```

```
<body>
    <form id="form1" runat="server">
    <div>
        <asp:Label ID="Label1" runat="server"
            Text="Please enter your name:" /><br />
        <asp:TextBox ID="TextBox1" runat="server" />
        <br /><br />
        <asp:Button ID="Button1" runat="server"
            Text="Submit" onclick="Button1_Click" />
    </div>
    </form>
</body>
</html>
```

4. Right-click in the code window and select **View Code** from the shortcut menu to switch to the code-behind file (WebForm1.aspx.cs). Replace the code in that file with the following:

```
using System;
namespace UsingSessionState
{
public partial class WebForm1
    : System.Web.UI.Page
{
        protected void Page_Load
        (object sender, EventArgs e)
        {
                if (Session["Name"] != null)
                    Response.Redirect("WebForm2.aspx");
        }

        protected void Button1_Click
            (object sender, EventArgs e)
        {
            Session.Add("Name", TextBox1.Text);
            Response.Redirect("WebForm2.aspx");
        }
    }
}
```

5. Add a new Web Form (WebForm2.aspx) to the project. Change the markup of the page to the following:

```
<%@ Page Language="C#" AutoEventWireup="true"
    CodeBehind="WebForm2.aspx.cs"
    Inherits="UsingSessionState.WebForm2" %>
<html xmlns="http://www.w3.org/1999/xhtml">
<head runat="server">
    <title></title>
```

```
    </head>
    <body>
        <form id="form1" runat="server">
        <div>
            <asp:Label ID="Label1" runat="server" /> <br />
            <asp:Button ID="Button1" runat="server"
                Text="Clear Session"
                onclick="Button1_Click" />
        </div>
        </form>
    </body>
    </html>
```

6. Change the code in the code-behind file (WebForm2.aspx.cs) for the form so that it reads as follows:

```
using System;
namespace UsingSessionState
{
    public partial class WebForm2
        : System.Web.UI.Page
    {
        protected void Page_Load(
            object sender, EventArgs e)
        {
            if (Session["Name"] != null)
                Label1.Text = String.Format(
                    "Welcome, {0}", Session["Name"]);
            else
                Response.Redirect("WebForm1.aspx");
        }
        protected void Button1_Click(
            object sender, EventArgs e)
        {
            Session.Remove("Name");
            Response.Redirect("WebForm1.aspx");
        }
    }
}
```

7. Select **Debug > Start Debugging** (or press **F5**). The WebForm1.aspx page will open in a Web browser, as shown in Figure 4-8. Enter a name and click the Submit button. This page stores the entered name in the session state.

**Figure 4-8**

This page stores the entered name in the session state

8. Next, you'll be transferred to WebForm2.aspx, as shown in Figure 4-9. WebForm2.aspx retrieves the user name from the session state. In the same browser window (so that you are within the same session), try accessing WebForm1.aspx. Notice that as long as the session contains an entry for the name, you will be redirected to WebForm2.aspx. Press the Clear Session button. This clears the session and transfers you to WebForm1.aspx.

**Figure 4-9**

This page retrieves the displayed name from the session
state

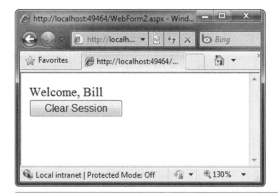

## ■ Understanding IIS Web Hosting

**THE BOTTOM LINE**

*Web hosting* involves setting up a Web server with correct code files and settings so that remote users can successfully access a Web application.

ASP.NET applications must be deployed on an Internet Information Services (IIS) Web server. IIS is an integral part of Windows Server operating systems and provides functionality for hosting Web sites.

Deploying an ASP.NET application is uncomplicated because ASP.NET provides xcopy deployment. What this means is that all you need to do to deploy an ASP.NET Web site to a Web server is copy the files to the correct locations. You can copy these files using either the Windows xcopy command or a File Transfer Protocol (FTP) application.

**TAKE NOTE***

Some complex Web applications may require you to deploy DLL files to the global assembly cache (GAC). In such situations, you may actually need to create a Windows Installer package for deployment rather than using xcopy or FTP.

## Understanding Internet Information Services

> *Internet Information Services (IIS)* is a Web server for hosting Web applications on the Windows operating system. An IIS server uses the concepts of sites, applications, and virtual directories.

You can use IIS to host multiple Web sites and share information with users over the Internet or over an intranet. IIS uses a hierarchical relationship among sites, applications, and virtual directories as a basic building block for hosting online content.

IIS can be administered using the IIS Manager tool, which is part of the Windows operating system. The IIS Manager tool, as shown in Figure 4-10, provides a graphical user interface to configure Web sites, applications, and virtual directories. The screenshot in Figure 4-10 is from a computer running Windows 7. The user interface of IIS Manager is different on Windows XP.

**Figure 4-10**

Internet Information Services (IIS) Manager interface on a computer running Windows 7

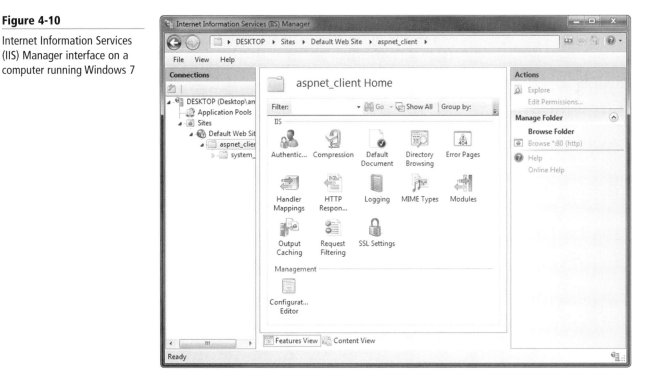

## Creating Virtual Directories and Web Sites

> A **Web site** is a container of applications and virtual directories. A *virtual directory* is an alias that maps to a physical directory on the Web server.

A Web site is a container of applications and virtual directories that can be accessed using a Web address. For example, the URL www.northwind.com may point to a Web site that has many virtual directories, such as orders and accounts, each of which can be accessed in combination with the Web site address—for example, via www.northwind.com/orders and www.northwind.com/account.

A Web server never exposes the actual physical address and location of files to the external world. Instead, it uses a system of aliases that map to the physical directories. These aliases are also called virtual directories. The virtual directories become a part of the URL, as demonstrated in the previous example. When IIS receives a request for such a URL, it maps the virtual directory to the physical location of the files. The following exercise shows how to create a virtual directory.

 **CREATE VIRTUAL DIRECTORY**

**GET READY.** To create a virtual directory using the IIS manager, take the following steps:

1. Open the IIS Manager. To open IIS Manager in Windows 7, type IIS in the Start menu, then click on the **Internet Information Service (IIS) Manager** shortcut. To access IIS Manager in Windows XP, go to **Start > Run**, type "inetmgr", and click the **OK** button.

2. Expand the nodes on the left panel (see Figure 4-10) and select the **Default Web Site node.**

3. Right-click on the **Default Web Site node** and select the **Add Virtual Directory** option from the shortcut menu. In Windows XP, the command will be **New > Virtual Directory**. At this point, a Virtual Directory Creation Wizard will appear on your screen.

4. In the Add Virtual Directory dialog box, provide an alias and physical path, as shown in Figure 4-11, then click **OK**.

**Figure 4-11**

Add Virtual Directory dialog box

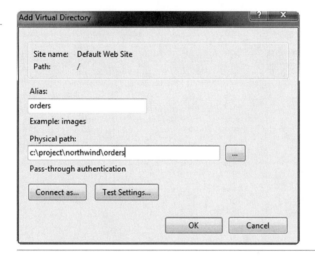

## Deploying Web Applications

> Deployment of simple Web sites is accomplished by copying the files to the correct location. To install a complex Web site, you may need to use Windows Installer.

There are two primary ways in which you can deploy files to a Web site:

- **Using xcopy or FTP:** Many Web applications and Web services simply require the files to be copied onto the Web server. These sites and services don't require any special actions, such as restarting IIS services, registering the components to Windows Registry, and so on. The xcopy or FTP deployment is ideal in such scenarios.

- **Using Windows Installer:** Windows Installer can perform a number of custom actions during the deployment process. Therefore, it can be used for deploying complex Web sites that require automatically creating virtual directories, restarting services, registering components, and so on.

# ■ Understanding Web Services Development

 **THE BOTTOM LINE**

A Web service is a software component that can be accessed over a network using standard network protocols such as HTTP. Web services are described using the Web services description language (WSDL).

*Web services* provide a way to interact with programming objects located on remote computers. What makes Web services special is that all communication between Web service servers and their clients occurs via Extensible Markup Language (XML) messages transmitted over the Hypertext Transfer Protocol (HTTP).

By using these standard technologies, remote objects can be published and consumed by otherwise noncompatible systems. For example, a remote object written in C# and published as a Web service on a Windows Web server can be processed by Java code running on a Linux machine.

Before we get into the details of creating and consuming Web services, let's familiarize ourselves with two key technologies that make Web services possible:

- *Simple Object Access Protocol (SOAP)*
- Web Services Description Language (WSDL)

## Introducing SOAP

SOAP is the protocol for exchanging structured information in a Web service communication between two remote computers.

SOAP is the protocol that defines how remote computers exchange messages as part of a Web service communication. SOAP relies on XML as its message format and uses HTTP for message transmission. Using SOAP to communicate has two major benefits. First, because Web service messages are formatted as XML, they're easier for noncompatible systems to understand. Second, because these messages are transmitted over the pervasive HTTP, they can normally reach any machine on the Internet without being blocked by firewalls.

Here's a typical SOAP packet sent from a client to a Web service:

```
<?xml version="1.0" encoding="utf-8"?>
<soap:Envelope
xmlns:xsi=http://www.w3.org/2001/XMLSchema-instance
xmlns:xsd=http://www.w3.org/2001/XMLSchema
xmlns:soap="http://schemas.xmlsoap.org/soap/envelope/">
  <soap:Body>
    <ToLower xmlns="http://northwindtraders.com">
      <inputString>SAMPLE STRING</inputString>
    </ToLower>
  </soap:Body>
</soap:Envelope>
```

As you look at the example, notice some of the obvious elements of this SOAP packet:

- The packet consists of an envelope that contains a body; each is identified with a specific XML tag.
- The body consists of the name of the method to be invoked. In this SOAP packet, the method name is ToLower, and it takes a single parameter by the name of inputString and a given value.

Here is the response packet from the server:

```
<?xml version="1.0" encoding="utf-8"?>
<soap:Envelope
xmlns:xsi="http://www.w3.org/2001/XMLSchema-instance"
xmlns:xsd="http://www.w3.org/2001/XMLSchema"
xmlns:soap="http://schemas.xmlsoap.org/soap/envelope/">
  <soap:Body>
    <ToLowerResponse
        xmlns="http://northwindtraders.com">
      <ToLowerResult>sample string</ToLowerResult>
    </ToLowerResponse>
  </soap:Body>
</soap:Envelope>
```

In the response packet, the ToLowerResponse XML element is the result of the method invocation on the server.

## Introducing WSDL

WSDL is an XML-based language for describing Web services.

WSDL stands for *Web services description language*, and it provides a standard by which a Web service can tell its client what kind of messages it will accept and what results will be returned. A WSDL file acts as the public interface of a Web service and includes the following information:

- The data types it can process
- The methods it exposes
- The URLs through which those methods can be accessed

## Creating Web Services

In this section, you learn how to create and publish a Web service.

In this section, you'll learn how to create a simple Web service called TextWebService that exposes two methods, ToLower and ToUpper. These methods convert a given string to lower-case and upper-case letters, respectively. Although this example is simple, it covers all aspects of creating a Web service that may involve more complex processing logic.

**CREATE A WEB SERVICE**

**GET READY.** To create a Web service, perform the following actions:

1.  Add a new project based on the ASP.NET Empty Web Application template to the Lesson04 solution. Name the project TextWebService, as shown in Figure 4-12.

**Figure 4-12**

Select the ASP.NET Empty Web Application template

2.  Select **Project > Add New Item** from the shortcut menu. Select the **Web Service template**, as shown in Figure 4-13. Name the Web service TextWebService.asmx.

**Figure 4-13**

Select the Web Service template

3.  Change the default code for the TextWebService class in the TextWebService.asmx.cs file as shown below:

[WebService(Namespace = "http://northwindtraders.com/")]

[WebServiceBinding(ConformsTo

    = WsiProfiles.BasicProfile1_1)]

public class TextWebService:

  System.Web.Services.WebService

```
        {
            [WebMethod]
            public string ToUpper(string inputString)
            {
                return inputString.ToUpper();
            }
            [WebMethod]
            public string ToLower(string inputString)
            {
                return inputString.ToLower();
            }
        }
    }
```

4. Select **Debug > Build TextWebService** to compile the project and ensure that there are no errors. The Web service is now ready for use.

 TAKE NOTE*

You can use your company's domain name as part of the namespace to distinguish your Web services from the services published by other companies.

In the above code, there are few important things to note. First, notice that each class that is exposed as an XML Web service needs to have a WebService attribute. The WebService attribute has a Namespace property that defaults to https://tempuri.org/. Although it is okay to have this value at development time, the namespace value should be changed before the Web service is published. In fact, each individual Web service must have a unique namespace in order for client applications to distinguish it from other Web services.

Each method that is exposed from the Web service also needs to have a WebMethod attribute. The methods marked with WebMethod attributes are also known as Web methods. The two methods used in this exercise convert a given string to upper-case and lower-case letters, respectively.

To test a simple Web service such as the TextWebService created above, all you need is a Web browser. You can select methods to invoke, pass parameters, and review the return values from within the browser, as shown in the following exercise.

 **TEST A WEB SERVICE**

**GET READY.** To test a Web service, perform the following tasks:

1. Open the TextWebService project that you created in the previous exercise. Select **Debug > Start Debugging**. A browser will be launched displaying the Web service test page, as shown in Figure 4-14.

**Figure 4-14**

Web service test page

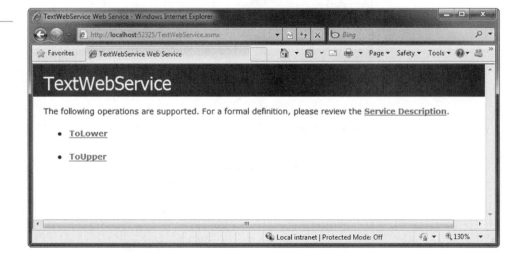

2. On the test page, click on the **Service Description** link. In this way, you will be able to view the WSDL for this Web service. Click on the **Back** button to return to the test page.

3. Notice that all the Web methods appear as links on the test page. To invoke a particular Web method, click on its link. After doing so, you should see a page for testing the selected Web method, as shown in Figure 4-15.

**Figure 4-15**

Web method test page

4. Each Web method test page shows the SOAP and other messages that the Web service understands. It also contains a form that allows you to enter method parameters and test the Web method. Enter a test input string and click the Invoke button. You should see a result on the next page, as shown in Figure 4-16.

**Figure 4-16**

Return value from the Web service test

5. Test both methods. When you are finished, close the Web browser.

As demonstrated in the exercise, when you click on the Invoke button, the test page constructs the appropriate SOAP packets for the Web service to process and then displays the results returned from the Web service.

## Consuming Web Services

In this section, you learn how to access Web services from a client application.

Earlier in the lesson, you learned how to invoke a Web service from the Web service test page. In this section, you'll learn how to call a Web service programmatically from within an ASP.NET client application.

 **ACCESS A WEB SERVICE FROM A CLIENT APPLICATION**

**GET READY.** To access a Web service from a client application, perform the following steps:

1. Add a new project to the solution Lesson04 based on the ASP.NET Web Application template. Name the project TextWebServiceClient.

2. Right-click the project's name in the Solution Explorer window, then select the **Add Web Reference** option from the shortcut menu. In the Add Web Reference dialog box, enter the URL of the service created in the previous exercise, and press **Enter.** (You can also copy the URL from the browser's address bar.) This action loads the list of operations available on the Web service, as shown in Figure 4-17.

**Figure 4-17**

Add Web Reference dialog box

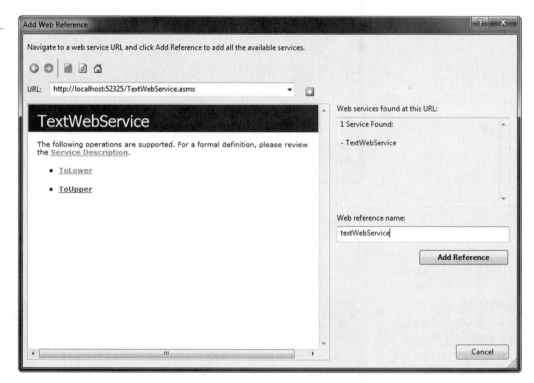

3. In the Add Web Reference dialog box, change the name of the Web reference to textWebService and click the **Add Reference** button. This will add a Web Reference to the project, as shown in Figure 4-18.

**Figure 4-18**

Web References Node for the project

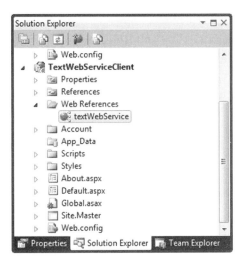

4. Change the code of the Default.aspx to the following:

```
<%@ Page Title="Home Page" Language="C#"
    AutoEventWireup="true"
    CodeBehind="Default.aspx.cs"
    Inherits="TextWebServiceClient._Default" %>
<html>
    <head><title>TextWebService Client
    </title></head>
  <body>
    <form runat="server">
        <h2>Test Form For TextWebService</h2>
        <p>
            <asp:TextBox ID="TextBox1"
                runat="server"
                Text="enter text" />
            <br />
            <asp:Button ID="Button1"
                runat="server"
                Text="Invoke Service Methods"
                onclick="Button1_Click" />
        </p>
        <p>
            <strong>Results:</strong><br />
            ToLower method:
            <asp:Label ID="toLowerLabel"
                runat="server"
                Text="Label" ForeColor="Green" />
            <br />
```

ToUpper method:
```
<asp:Label ID="toUpperLabel"
    runat="server"
    Text="Label" ForeColor="Green" />
```
       `</p>`
    `</form>`
  `</body>`
`</html>`

5. Open the Design view for Default.aspx and double-click the **Button** control. This adds code for the Click event handler. Modify the code as shown below:

```
protected void Button1_Click(
    object sender, EventArgs e)
{

    var webService =
        new textWebService.TextWebService();
    toLowerLabel.Text =
        webService.ToLower(TextBox1.Text);
    toUpperLabel.Text =
        webService.ToUpper(TextBox1.Text);
}
```

6. Select **Debug > Start Debugging** to run the Web application. Enter some sample text, then click the Invoke Service Methods button. You should see the results from the TextWebService, as shown in Figure 4-19.

**Figure 4-19**

Return value from the Web service

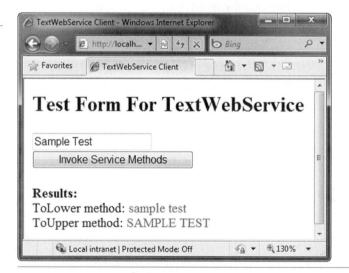

In the above exercise, when you add a Web reference, Visual Studio creates a local proxy that represents the remote service. The proxy simplifies communication with the Web service by accepting messages, forwarding them to the Web service, and returning results from the Web service.

You can easily use this proxy to create objects from the Web service and invoke methods. As a result, working with remote objects is similar to working with local objects.

When you create a Web reference, Visual Studio reads the appropriate WSDL file to determine which classes and methods are available on the remote server. When you call a method on a remote object, the .NET Framework translates your call and results into SOAP messages and transmits them with no intervention on your part.

## SKILL SUMMARY

**IN THIS LESSON, YOU LEARNED THE FOLLOWING:**

- A Web page is a document that is served over the World Wide Web (WWW) and can be displayed by a Web browser.
- Hypertext Markup Language (HTML) is the language used by Web servers and browsers to describe a Web page.
- Cascading style sheets (CSS) enable you to store style and formatting information separate from HTML code. This separation makes it easy to update a Web site. Visual Studio includes tools to build and preview your style sheets.
- JavaScript is a client-side scripting language that runs inside a Web browser to help create far more interactive Web pages than are possible with only HTML.
- Client-side state management techniques such as query strings, cookies, hidden fields, and ViewState use HTML and the capabilities of Web browsers to store state information on client computers.
- Server-side state management techniques such as session state and application state use server resources for state management.
- Internet Information Services (IIS) is a Web server for hosting Web applications on the Windows operating system. An IIS server uses the concepts of sites, applications, and virtual directories.
- Web services provide a way to invoke remote objects using standard technologies such as XML and HTTP.
- SOAP is the protocol that defines how remote computers exchange messages as part of Web service communication. SOAP relies on XML for its message format and uses HTTP for message transmission.
- WSDL provides a standard by which a Web service can tell its client what kinds of messages it will accept and what results will be returned.

## Knowledge Assessment

### Fill in the Blank

*Complete the following sentences by writing the correct word or words in the blanks provided.*

1. In the HTML anchor tag (<a>), the _____ attribute specifies the target URL.

2. You can put CSS code in a separate file and link it to a Web page through use of the HTML _____ element.

3. The JavaScript code on a Web page is executed on the _____.

4. You can use a(n) _____ element to display a specific message to users when their browser is not running JavaScript.

5. You can disable ViewState at the page level by setting the _____ attribute of the Page directive to false in the ASP.NET page.

6. The _____ state is used to store data that is used globally throughout an application, as opposed to the _____ state, which stores data for a user session.

7. A Web application is accessed using a(n) _____ name instead of a physical folder name.

8. You must mark classes with the _____ attribute to expose them as a Web service.

9. Of all the methods in a Web service class, only those marked with _____ attributes are exposed as Web service methods.

10. SOAP relies on _____ as its message format and uses _____ for message transmission.

## Multiple Choice

*Circle the letter that corresponds to the best answer.*

1. You write the following code for your Web page:

```
<html>
    <head>
        <title>Sample Page</title>
        <style type="text/css">
        div
        {
            font-family: Verdana;
            font-size: 9pt;
        }
        </style>
    </head>
    <body>
        <div style=
            "font-weight: bold; font-size: 12pt;">
        Sample Text</div>
    </body>
</html>
```

What would be the style for text displayed as part of the <div> element?
a. Font family: Verdana; font weight: bold; font size: 12pt
b. Font family: Verdana; font weight: bold; font size: 9pt
c. Font family: Verdana; font size: 12pt
d. Font family: Verdana; font size: 9pt

2. You are developing a mapping Web site that allows users to interactively explore maps using actions such as panning and zooming. You want the Web site to be responsive and accessible in most modern Web browsers. However, you do not want users to need to install additional plug-ins in order to use your Web site. Which of the following technologies should you use to display maps?
   a. HTML
   b. Server-side programming technology such as ASP.NET
   c. Adobe Flash
   d. JavaScript

3. Your ASP.NET page contains a page-level variable of Customer type. You want to pre-serve the value of this variable across page postbacks, but you do not need this variable in any other page in the application. Which of the following state-management techniques is the best way to achieve this?
   a. Query strings
   b. Cookies
   c. ViewState
   d. Session

4. You are developing a Web application for an online bank. Your application enables users to access their account information and transactions from within a Web browser. When a user logs onto the Web application, you want to show the username and account balance on all pages of the application until the user logs off. You also want this application to be safe from malicious users. Which of the following state-management techniques should you use?
   a. Cookies
   b. ViewState
   c. ViewState with encryption
   d. Session

5. You are developing a Web form to display weather information. When a user requests the Web form, the form needs to perform some initialization to change its appearance and assign values to some controls. Where should you put the code?
   a. In the PreInit event handler of the Page class
   b. In the Init event handler of the Page class
   c. In the Load event handler of the Page class
   d. In the PreRender event handler of the Page class

6. You want to display values of the C# expressions in an ASP.NET page. Which of the following types of code blocks should you use to enclose the expression?
   a. <script runat="server">...</script>
   b. <script>...</script>
   c. <%= ... %>
   d. <form>...</form>

7. You have developed a timesheet application that will be used by all employees in your company. You used ASP.NET to develop this application and have deployed it on the company's Web server. What must all employees of the company install on their computers before they can access the timesheet application?
   a. .NET Framework Redistributable
   b. .NET Framework Software Development Kit
   c. Visual Studio
   d. A Web browser

8. Your client application calls for a Web service that performs complex, time-consuming calculations. A user complains that while results are being returned, the user interface freezes momentarily. Which approach should you take to solve this issue?
   a. You should install a better processor on the Web server.
   b. You should install a better processor on the client computer.
   c. You should upgrade to a faster Internet connection.
   d. You should use asynchronous calls to invoke the Web service.

9. You have created an ASP.NET Web service that converts one currency into another. One of the methods in your Web service is defined with the following code:

   ```
   public double Convert(double amount,

        string from, string to)

   {

        // code to perform currency conversion

   }
   ```

   The users of the Web service report that they can set a reference to the Web service but the Convert method is not available to them. What could be the problem?
   a. The .asmx file for the Web service is not available on the Web server.
   b. The Web service class is not marked with the WebService attribute.
   c. The Convert method is not marked with the WebMethod attribute.
   d. Web services can only expose methods that return text values.

10. You are working on two Visual Studio projects. The first project is a Web service that returns a DataSet object belonging to the System.Data namespace. The second project accesses the Web service created by the first project. Which project in this scenario requires a reference to the System.Data namespace?
    a. The Web service project
    b. The client project that accesses the Web service
    c. Both the client project and the Web service project
    d. Neither the client project nor the Web service project

## ■ Competency Assessment

### Scenario 4-1: Using JavaScript and HTML

You are developing a Web page that provides a responsive user interface. You decide to display an image on the page. When the user moves his or her mouse over the image, the original image is replaced with a new image. Then, when the mouse moves out of the image area, the original image is displayed again. You hope to accomplish this using client-side JavaScript and HTML code. How would you create a Web page that works as described here?

### Scenario 4-2: Using Query Strings

You are developing a portion of a Web site that allows users to enter their name and email address to subscribe to an email newsletter. Your solution consists of two Web pages. The first page collects the user name and email address and then transfers control to a second page. The second page accepts the name and the email address as query-string parameters and displays a confirmation message to the user. You need to write code for these two pages. What code will you write to accomplish this requirement?

### Scenario 4-3: Calling a Web Service Asynchronously

The proxy class generated by Visual Studio for a Web service includes methods for calling the Web service synchronously as well as asynchronously. By default, the application uses the synchronous method. If you prefer asynchronous invocation, you need to call the asynchronous version of the method. The asynchronous versions do not wait for the Web service to return a response and use a callback mechanism to get a response when it is ready. Asynchronous invocation of a Web service may help client applications be more responsive. If you want to call the ToLower method of the previously created TextWebService in an asynchronous fashion. What code would you write for asynchronously invoking a Web service?

### Scenario 4-4: Using Session State

You are developing a portion of a Web site that allows users to enter their name and email address to subscribe to an email newsletter. Your solution consists of two Web pages. The first page collects the user name and email address, adds them to the session state, and transfers control to a second page. The second page retrieves the name and the email address from the session state and displays a confirmation message. You need to write code for these two pages. What code will you write to accomplish this requirement?

# 5 LESSON

# Understanding Desktop Applications

## LESSON SKILL MATRIX

| SKILLS/CONCEPTS | MTA EXAM OBJECTIVE | MTA EXAM OBJECTIVE NUMBER |
| --- | --- | --- |
| Understanding Objects | Understand Windows Forms applications. | 5.1 |
| Understanding Values and References | Understand console-based applications. | 5.2 |
| Understanding Encapsulation | Understand Windows services. | 5.3 |

## KEY TERMS

command-line parameters

console-based application

delegates

events

installer

Multiple Document
   Interface (MDI) applications

visual inheritance

Windows Forms applications

Windows service

You are a software developer for a large business organization. You need to develop an application that integrates closely with the user's Windows desktop and provides a user interface similar to that of popular desktop applications on the Windows platform. The application needs to be functional whether it is connected to or disconnected from the network. The application should also be able to communicate with devices such as hand-held scanners and printers.

## ■ Understanding Windows Forms Applications

**THE BOTTOM LINE**

*Windows Forms applications* are smart client applications consisting of one or more forms that display a visual interface to the user. These applications integrate well with the operating system, use connected devices, and can work whether connected to the Internet or not.

## Designing a Windows Form

> A Windows Form is a visual surface capable of displaying a variety of controls, including text boxes, buttons, and menus. Visual Studio provides a drag-and-drop Windows Forms designer that you can use to easily create your applications.

To design Windows Forms, you must first decide what controls you want to place on the form. Windows Forms provides a large collection of common controls that you can readily use to create an excellent user interface. If the functionality you are looking for is not already available as a common control, you have the option to either create a custom control yourself or buy a control from a third-party vendor.

You can use the functionality provided by Visual Studio's Windows Forms Designer to quickly place and arrange controls per your requirements. Visual Studio provides easy access to the available controls through its toolbox, as shown in Figure 5-1.

**Figure 5-1**

Visual Studio toolbox

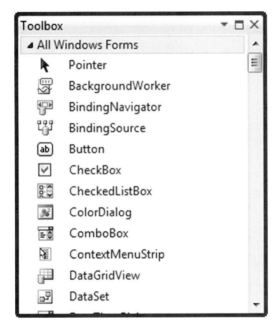

A form and its components generally respond to user actions such as keystrokes or mouse movement. These actions are called *events*. Much of the code that you write as a Windows Forms developer is directed toward capturing such events and handling them by creating an appropriate response. For instance, in the following exercise, you will create a Windows Form that displays the date value selected by the user.

 **CREATE A WINDOWS FORM**

**GET READY.** Launch Microsoft Visual Studio. Then, perform the following actions:

1. Create a new project based on the Windows Forms Application template, as shown in Figure 5-2. Name the project WindowsFormsDesign.

**Figure 5-2**

Visual Studio New Project dialog box

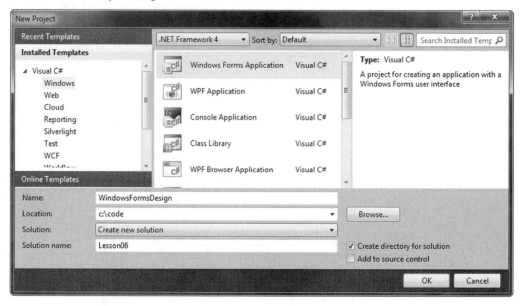

2. The Windows Form Application project will load with a default form (Form1.cs) opened in the Designer view. The Designer view allows you to work visually with the form. For example, you can arrange controls on the form's surface and set their properties. Available controls can be accessed from the Toolbox window. If you don't already see the Toolbox window, select **View > Toolbox** to display it. Then, from the Toolbox, drag and drop a DateTimePicker control and a Label control on the Designer surface and arrange the controls as shown in Figure 5-3.

**Figure 5-3**

Windows Form with a DateTimePicker control and a Label control

3. In the Designer view, select the **Label** control and, using the Properties window, set its **Text** property to an empty string.

4. Also in the Designer view, double-click the **DateTimePicker** control. This action attaches the default event handler for the ValueChanged event of the DateTimePicker control and switches the view from Designer to Code. Next, change the default code for the event handler as follows:

```
private void dateTimePicker1_ValueChanged
        (object sender, EventArgs e)
{
    label1.Text =
        dateTimePicker1.Value.ToLongDateString();
}
```

**TAKE NOTE** ✱

In this exercise, we used the default control names. In complex forms with more controls, it's always a good idea to give the controls more meaningful names.

5. Select **Debug > Start Debugging** (or press **F5**) to run the project. On the user interface, select a new date and verify that the selected date is displayed on the Label control.

In this exercise, note that when the form is initially displayed, the Label control is set to an empty string. Then, as soon as you change the date selection by manipulating the DateTimePicker control, the selected date value is set as the text for the Label control.

## Understanding the Windows Form Event Model

Event handling plays a key role in user interface-based programming; through event handling, you respond to various events that are fired as a result of user actions and thus make programs interactive. The Windows Forms event model uses .NET Framework *delegates* to bind events to their respective event handlers.

In Windows Forms applications, each form and control exposes a predefined set of events. When an event occurs, the code in the associated event handler is invoked. For instance, in the previous exercise, when you double-clicked the DateTimePicker control to add code to the event handler, Visual Studio generated the following code to attach the event handler to the event:

```
this.dateTimePicker1.ValueChanged +=
    new System.EventHandler(
    this.dateTimePicker1_ValueChanged);
```

**TAKE NOTE** ✱

A delegate can be bound to any method whose signature matches that of the event handler.

Here, ValueChanged is the event of the DateTimePicker control that we want to capture. So, a new instance of the delegate of type EventHandler is created and the method dateTimePicker1_ValueChanged is passed to the event handler. The dateTimePicker1_ValueChanged method is the method in which you will actually write the event-handling code.

This code is automatically generated by the Visual Studio Designer. You will find this code in the code-behind file for the designer (Form1.Designer.cs), inside a code region entitled Windows Form Designer generated code.

Yet another thing to notice is that the syntax for adding a delegate uses the += operator. That's because the .NET Framework supports multicast delegates in which a delegate can be bound to more than one method, thus allowing one-to-many notifications when an event is fired.

## Using Visual Inheritance

*Visual inheritance* allows you to reuse existing functionality and layout for Windows Forms.

One of the core principles of object-oriented programming is inheritance. When a class inherits from a base class, it derives its base functionality from the base class. Of course, you can always extend the derived class to provide additional functionality and be more useful.

A Windows Form, at its core, is just another class; therefore, inheritance applies to it as well. However, when inheritance is applied to a Windows Form, it causes the inheritance of all the visual characteristics of a form, such as size, color, and any controls placed on the form. You can also visually manipulate any of the properties that are inherited from the base class. Therefore, inheriting Windows Forms is often called *visual inheritance*. In the following exercise, you will create a Windows Form via visual inheritance of an existing form.

 **CREATE A WINDOWS FORM USING VISUAL INHERITANCE**

**GET READY.** Launch Microsoft Visual Studio and open the existing Windows Application Project named WindowsFormsDesign. Then, perform these steps:

1. Open Form1.designer.cs and change the access modifiers for the label1 and dateTimePicker1 controls from private to protected, as shown:

   ```
   protected System.Windows.Forms.Label label1;
   protected System.Windows.Forms.DateTimePicker
       dateTimePicker1;
   ```

2. Select **Project > Add Windows Forms** to add a new Windows Form based on the Inherited Form template. You can quickly search for this template by typing its name in the search box, as shown in Figure 5-4. Name the inherited form InheritedForm.cs. (Note that the Inherited Form template is not available in Visual Studio Express editions. If you are using an Express edition, just create a regular Windows Form named InheritedForm.cs and proceed to Step 4.)

**Figure 5-4**

Inherited Form template

3. Click the **Add** button. Then, in the Inheritance Picker dialog box, select **Form1** from the WindowsFormsDesign namespace, as shown in Figure 5-5, and click the **OK** button.

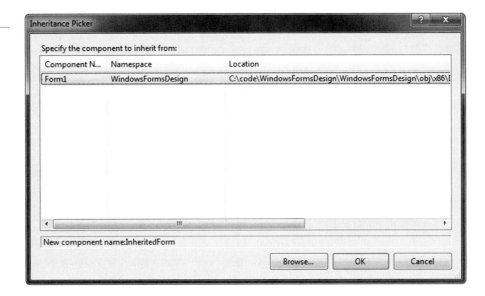

4. Select the **Code view** for the InheritedForm; you will see that the class InheritedForm inherits from Form1, as shown below. If you did not use the Inherited Form template in Step 2, you'll need to manually modify the code to add the code for inheritance (shown in bold):

```
public partial class InheritedForm
    : WindowsFormsDesign.Form1
{
      public InheritedForm()
      {
         InitializeComponent();
      }
}
```

5. In the Designer view of the InheritedForm, set the Text property to **Inherited Form**.
6. Also in the Designer view, double-click **InheritedForm**. This action attaches an event handler for the Load event of the form and switches the view from Designer to Code. In Code view, change the default code for the event handler as follows:

```
private void InheritedForm_Load(
    object sender, EventArgs e)
{
    label1.Text =
      dateTimePicker1.Value.ToLongDateString();
}
```

7. Open Program.cs and modify the Main method as shown below to make sure that InheritedForm is launched when you run the application:

```
[STAThread]
static void Main()
{
    Application.EnableVisualStyles();
    Application
      .SetCompatibleTextRenderingDefault(false);
    Application.Run(new InheritedForm());
}
```

8. Select **Debug > Start Debugging** (or press **F5**) to run the project. When InheritedForm is loaded, the currently selected date is displayed on the Label control. This is unlike the previously created Form1, in which the Label control was initially empty.

The InheritedForm form demonstrates that you can get all of Form1's functionality simply by inheriting the form. When you change the access modifier of Form1's member controls, label1 and dateTimePicker1, from private to protected, you will be able to access them from within the inherited form. This exercise also demonstrates how you can extend the functionality of the base form in an inherited form.

## Understanding Multiple Document Interface (MDI) Applications

*Multiple Document Interface (MDI) applications* are applications in which multiple child windows reside under a single parent window.

MDI applications allow multiple windows to share a single application menu and toolbar. MDI applications often have a menu named Window that allows users to manage multiple child windows, offering features such as switching between child windows and arranging child windows. For example, Figure 5-6 shows Microsoft Excel 2010 in MDI mode.

**Figure 5-6**

Microsoft Excel 2010 as an MDI application

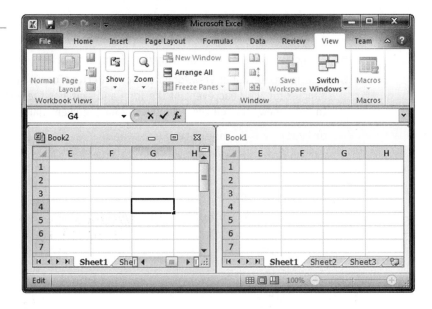

MDI applications contrast with single document interface (SDI) applications in which each window contains its own menu and toolbar. SDI applications rely on the operating system to provide window management functionality. For example, in Windows, you can switch among multiple windows by using the Windows Taskbar.

There is much debate among user-interface designers as to which application interface works best. Generally speaking, SDI is considered more suited to novice users, whereas MDI is considered more suited to advanced users. Many popular applications such as Microsoft Word and Microsoft Excel support both SDI and MDI. Word and Excel install by default as SDI applications, but they provide users with an option to switch between SDI and MDI. For example, in Word 2010 and Excel 2010, you can switch to MDI mode by unchecking the "Show all windows in the Taskbar" option in the Options menu.

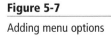

**TAKE NOTE** *

It can be tricky to implement support for multiple monitors in MDI applications because the parent window needs to span all of the user's monitors.

 **CREATE AN MDI APPLICATION**

**GET READY.** Launch Microsoft Visual Studio and create a new Windows Forms Application Project named MDIApplication. Then, perform these steps:

1. Select the Properties window for Form1 and set the **Text** property to **MDI Application** and the **IsMdiContainer** property to True.

2. Select the **MenuStrip** control from the Toolbox and add it to the form. Add a top-level menu item **&Window**, and then add **&New Window** and **&Arrange** at the next level. Under the Arrange menu, add three options—**&Cascade**, **&Horizontal**, and **&Vertical**—as shown in Figure 5-7.

**Figure 5-7**

Adding menu options

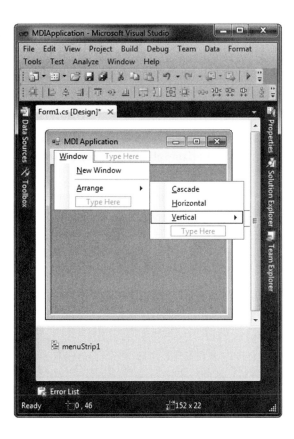

> **TAKE NOTE ***
> The & sign in front of a character in a menu's text is not displayed as is; rather, it sets the character to be the shortcut key for the menu. For example, the &Window menu can be invoked by pressing Alt+W. The access keys will not be evident until the user presses the Alt key. A setting in the Windows operating system controls whether access keys are always visible.

3. For the MenuStrip control, set its **MdiWindowListItem** property to the name of the Window menu (windowToolStripMenuItem by default).

4. In the Solutions Explorer, right-click the project and select **Add > Windows Form**. Add a new Windows Form with the name **ChildForm**.

5. Double-click the child form and add the following code to handle the Load event:

```
private void ChildForm_Load(
    object sender, EventArgs e)
{
    Text = DateTime.Now.ToString();
}
```

6. On the parent form, double-click the **Window > New Window** menu item and add the following event handler for its Click event:

```
private void newWindowToolStripMenuItem_Click(
    object sender, EventArgs e)
{
ChildForm child = new ChildForm();
child.MdiParent = this;
child.Show();
}
```

7. On the parent form, double-click **Window > Arrange, Window > Cascade, Window > Arrange, Window > Horizontal**, and **Window > Arrange, Window > Vertical**, respectively, and add the following event handlers for their Click events:

```
private void cascadeToolStripMenuItem_Click(
    object sender, EventArgs e)
{
    LayoutMdi(MdiLayout.Cascade);
}
private void horizontalToolStripMenuItem_Click(
    object sender, EventArgs e)
{
    LayoutMdi(MdiLayout.TileHorizontal);
}
private void verticalToolStripMenuItem_Click(
    object sender, EventArgs e)
{
    LayoutMdi(MdiLayout.TileVertical);
}
```

8. Select **Debug > Start Debugging** (or press **F5**) to run the project. Select **Window > New Window** to create multiple new child windows. Switch among the child windows. Note that there is only one application instance in the Windows Taskbar. Now, use the options in the **Window > Arrange** menu to arrange the child windows. For example, an application with three child windows might look like the image in Figure 5-8 when the child windows are arranged horizontally.

**Figure 5-8**

An MDI application with three horizontally arranged child windows

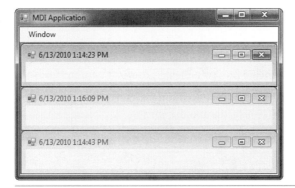

Let's review some of the important properties and methods used in this exercise. First, for the parent form, the IsMdiContainer property is set to true. This property indicates that the form is a container for multiple MDI child forms. Correspondingly, for each child form, you set the MdiParent property to specify the parent container form.

Next, the MdiWindowListItem property of the MenuStrip is used to indicate which menu item will be used to display the list of MDI child windows. When this property is set, the menu item will list all the child windows and also allow you to switch among child windows. As a result of the code in the ChildForm_Load method, the title bar for each form displays the date and time of the instant when the form was loaded.

Finally, the LayoutMdi method is used by the menu items in the Window menu to arrange the child windows. The method accepts a parameter of type MdiLayout enumeration. The enumeration value determines whether the child windows need to be tiled horizontally or vertically, cascaded, or displayed as icons.

**CERTIFICATION READY**
Do you understand how to develop Windows Forms applications?
5.1

## ■ Understanding Console-Based Applications

**THE BOTTOM LINE**

*Console-based applications* do not have a graphical user interface and use a text-mode console window to interact with the user. These applications are best suited for tasks that require minimal or no user interface.

**TAKE NOTE***

To enable reading from or writing to the console from a Windows Forms application, set the project's Output Type to Console Application in the project's Properties.

As its name suggests, a console-based application is run from the console window. The input to this application can be provided using *command-line parameters*, or the application can interactively read characters from the console window. Similarly, the output of a console application is written to the command window as well. You can enable reading or writing to the console by creating an application using the Console Application template in Visual Studio.

You can also use console-based applications to create commands that can be run from the command line. For example, you can take advantage of the pipes and filters provided by the operating system to pass the output of a command as input to another command, thereby creating more powerful commands by combining simple commands.

## Working with Command-Line Parameters

In this section, you'll learn how to accept command-line parameters from a console application.

The following exercise creates a simple console application that accepts the name of a text file as a command-line argument and displays the contents of that file.

 **CREATE A CONSOLE APPLICATION**

**GET READY.** Launch Microsoft Visual Studio. Then, perform these steps:

1. Create a new project based on the Console Application template, as shown in Figure 5-9. Name the project DisplayFile.

**Figure 5-9**

Console Application template

2. In the Program.cs, modify the code inside the Main method as shown below:

```
static void Main(string[] args)
{
    if (args.Length < 1)
        return;
    string[] lines = File.ReadAllLines(args[0]);
    foreach (string item in lines)
    {
        Console.WriteLine(item);
    }
}
```

3. Add the following using directive to the file:

```
using System.IO;
```

4. Select **Build > Build Solution** (or press **F6**) to build the Project.

5. Create a text file using Visual Studio or Notepad, enter some sample text, and save the file as Sample.txt in the same folder as the executable file. (The executable file is created by default in the bin\debug folder under the project's folder.)

6. Open a command prompt and navigate to the path of the project's EXE file. Execute the following command:

```
DisplayFile sample.txt
```

This command should display the contents of the text file in the command window.

7. Alternatively, you can also pass the command line argument from within Visual Studio by using the Project's Properties window, as shown in Figure 5-10. To view the project's Properties window, select the **Project > DisplayFile Properties** menu option.

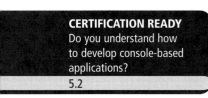

**Figure 5-10**

Setting start options in the project's Properties window

## Understanding Windows Services

**THE BOTTOM LINE**

A **Windows service** is an application that runs in the background and does not have any user interface.

The nature of Windows services make them ideal for creating long-running programs that run in the background and do not directly provide any user interaction. A Windows service can be started, paused, restarted, and stopped. A Windows service can also be set to start automatically when the computer is started.

Some examples of Windows services include a Web server that listens for incoming requests and sends a response, or an operating system's print spooler that provides printing services to the application programs.

Services play an important role in enterprise application architecture. For example, you can have a service that listens for incoming orders and starts an order-processing workflow whenever an order is received.

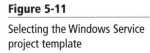 **TAKE NOTE**

> Because a Windows service is capable of running in the background, it does not need a logged-on user in order to function. Windows services will run in their own Windows session in the specified security context. Still, depending on what permissions are needed, you can specify a user account under which to run the service.

## Creating a Windows Service

> To create a Windows service in Visual Studio, use the Windows Service application template. Note that a Windows service must be installed before it can be used.

**TAKE NOTE** *

Visual Studio Express Edition does not provides templates for creating Windows service projects. Thus, you will need a non-express version of Visual Studio to complete exercises that use Windows service projects.

All Windows services must derive from the ServiceBase class. This base class provides the basic structure and functionality for creating a Windows service. You can override the base class methods OnStart, OnStop, OnPause, and OnContinue to add your own custom logic that executes in response to changes in service states.

The following exercise demonstrates how to create a simple Windows service that writes messages to the Application event log. Event logs are the part of Windows that is used by operating system tasks and applications running in the background to log error or other informational messages. Windows define three event logs by default: System, Application, and Security. Applications usually use the Application event log to log their message. The Windows Event Viewer utility can be used to view the messages in event logs.

### → CREATE A WINDOWS SERVICE

**GET READY.** Launch Microsoft Visual Studio. Then, perform these steps:

1. Create a new project based on the Windows Service template. Name the project FirstService, as shown in Figure 5-11.

**Figure 5-11**

Selecting the Windows Service project template

2. Select the **Properties** window for Service1 and set the **(Name)** and **ServiceName** properties to "FirstService".

3. In the Solution Explorer, rename the file Service1.cs as FirstService.cs. Open Program.cs and verify that the references to Service1 have been changed to FirstService.

4. Select the **Properties** window for the service and set the **CanPauseAndContinue** property and the **CanShutdown** property to **True**.

5. Open the designer for FirstService and add an EventLog component to it from the Toolbox. The EventLog component allows you to connect with the event logs.

6. View the code for FirstService and modify the constructor as shown below. In this code, you first create an event source by the name FirstService. This event source is used to distinguish messages generated by a specific application from all other messages in an event log. Then, you set the Source property of the event log component to the name of the event source. The Log property of the event log component, eventLog1, is used to specify the event log used to record the messages:

```
public FirstService()
{
    InitializeComponent();
    if (!EventLog.SourceExists("FirstService"))
    {
        EventLog.CreateEventSource(
            "FirstService", "Application");
    }
    eventLog1.Source = "FirstService";
    eventLog1.Log = "Application";
}
```

7. Add the following code to the service state change methods to define their behavior. The WriteEntry method of the event log component, eventLog1, is used to write a message to an event log. As part of the method, you can specify the type of message. For example, your message can be an error message, a warning message, or just a piece of information:

```
protected override void OnStart(string[] args)
{
    eventLog1.WriteEntry(
      "Starting the service",
      EventLogEntryType.Information, 1001);
}

protected override void OnStop()
{
    eventLog1.WriteEntry(
      "Stopping the service",
      EventLogEntryType.Information, 1001);
}
```

```
protected override void OnPause()
{
    eventLog1.WriteEntry(
      "Pausing the service",
      EventLogEntryType.Information, 1001);
}
protected override void OnContinue()
{
    eventLog1.WriteEntry(
      "Continuing the service",
      EventLogEntryType.Information, 1001);
}
protected override void OnShutdown()
{
    eventLog1.WriteEntry(
      "Shutting down the service",
      EventLogEntryType.Information, 1001);
}
```

8. Select **Build > Build Solution** (or press **F6**) to build the project.

Here, the code for FirstService overrides the OnStart, OnStop, OnPause, OnContinue, and OnShutdown methods to write messages to the event log. Not all services need to override these methods, however. Whether a service needs to override these methods depends on the value of the CanPauseAndContinue and CanShutdown properties of the Windows service.

The eventlog's WriteEntry method takes the message to write to the log, the type of event log entry (information, error, warning, etc.), and an eventId, which is an application-specific id used to identify the event.

The FirstService Windows service is now ready, but before it can be used, it must be installed in the Windows service database. This is done by adding a Service Installer to the Windows service project. The following exercise shows how to do this.

 **ADD AN INSTALLER TO A WINDOWS SERVICE**

**GET READY.** Launch Microsoft Visual Studio. Then, perform these steps:

1. Open the FirstService project created in the previous exercise. Right-click the **Designer surface** of FirstService.cs and select the **Add Installer** option from the context menu.

2. This action adds a new file ProjectInstaller.cs to the project. Open the Designer for ProjectInstaller.cs. You should see that two components were added to the Designer, as shown in Figure 5-12.

**Figure 5-12**

Designer view for ProjectInstaller.cs

3. Access the properties for the serviceProcessInstaller1component, and change the Account property to LocalService.

4. Next, access the properties for the serviceInstaller1component. Change the **DisplayName** property to FirstService and the **Description** property to "A simple test service." Note that the value of the StartType property is set by default to Manual.

5. Select **Build > Build Solution** (or press **F6**) to build the project. The Windows service is now ready to be installed.

**TAKE NOTE***

The StartType property of the ServiceInstaller class indicates how and when a service is started. The StartType property can have one of three possible values. The value Manual, which is also the default value, indicates that you need to start the service manually. The value Automatic indicates that the service will be started automatically when Windows is started. The value Disabled indicates that the service cannot be started.

**TAKE NOTE***

To minimize security risks, you should refrain from using the LocalSystem account for running a Windows service unless that service requires higher security privileges to function.

When you add an *installer* to a Windows Service project, the ServiceProcessInstaller and the ServiceInstaller classes are added to the project. The ServiceProcessInstaller class performs installation tasks that are common to all the Windows services in an application. This includes setting the login account for the Windows service. The ServiceInstaller class, on the other hand, performs the installation tasks that are specific to a single Windows service, such as setting the ServiceName and StartType.

The Account property of the ServiceProcessInstaller class specifies the type of account under which the services run. The Account property is of the type ServiceAccount enumeration where the possible values are LocalService, LocalSystem, NetworkService, and User. The LocalSystem value specifies a highly privileged account, whereas the LocalService account acts as a nonprivileged user.

An executable file that has the code for the service installer classes can be installed by using the command line Installer tool (installutil.exe). The following exercise shows how to install a Windows service application in the Windows service database.

 **INSTALL A WINDOWS SERVICE**

**GET READY.** To install a Windows service, take the following steps:

1. Run Visual Studio Command Prompt as administrator. To access the command prompt, go to **Start > All Programs > Visual Studio > Visual Studio Tools**, then choose **Visual Studio Command Prompt**. To run a program as administrator in Windows, right-click on the program shortcut and select the **Run as administrator** option from the shortcut menu.

2. Change the directory to the output directory of the FirstService project. This is the directory where the executable file is located.

3. Issue the following command; you should see results like those shown in Figure 5-13:

```
installutil FirstService.exe
```

**Figure 5-13**

Using installutil.exe

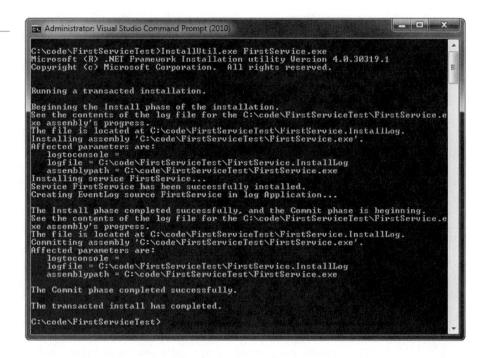

4. The Windows service FirstService is now installed.

**TAKE NOTE***

Installing a Windows service requires access to Windows Registry. Therefore, be sure to run installUtil.exe as an administrator.

The Windows service application is now stored in the Windows service database. Earlier, when you added a ServiceInstaller for the FirstService, you set the StartType property of the serviceInstaller1 component to Manual. As a result, you'll need to manually start the service when needed. The following exercise demonstrates how to start, pause, continue, and stop a Windows service.

 **WORK WITH A WINDOWS SERVICE**

**TAKE NOTE***

To uninstall a Windows service, use InstallUtil. exe with the option -u.

**GET READY.** Launch the Computer Management window by right-clicking **My Computer** and selecting **Manage** from the shortcut menu. Then, perform these steps:

1. In the Computer Management window, expand the **Services** and **Applications** section and select **Services**. A list of all services installed on the computer should be displayed, as shown in Figure 5-14.

**Figure 5-14**

The Services section allows you to work with installed services

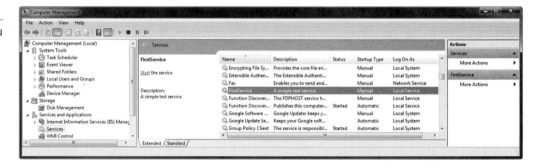

2. Select the **FirstService** service and click on the **Start** hyperlink, as shown in Figure 5-14. You should see a dialog box indicating progress, as shown in Figure 5-15. When the service is started, the status of the service will change to Started.

**Figure 5-15**

Service Control message when starting a service

3. Expand the **Event Viewer** node and select the **Application Windows** log. You should see a message from FirstService that says "Starting the Service," as shown in Figure 5-16.

**Figure 5-16**

The Application Windows Log

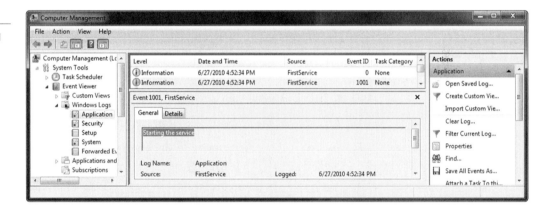

**CERTIFICATION READY**
Do you understand how to develop Windows services?
5.3

4. Go back to the list of Services and attempt to pause, resume, or stop FirstService. Check the Application event log to verify that the appropriate messages are being displayed.

In the last few exercises, you saw how to create, install, and use a Windows service. You also learned how to programmatically add messages to the Windows Application event log.

## SKILL SUMMARY

**IN THIS LESSON, YOU LEARNED THE FOLLOWING:**

- A Windows Form is a visual surface that can display a variety of controls, such as text boxes, buttons, and menus. Visual Studio provides a drag-and-drop Windows Forms designer that you can use to create applications.

- In Windows Forms, each form and control exposes a predefined set of events. When an event occurs, the code in the associated event handler is invoked. The Windows Forms event model uses .NET Framework delegates to bind events to their respective event handlers.

- Visual inheritance allows you to reuse existing functionality and layout for Windows Forms.

- Multiple document interface (MDI) applications are applications in which multiple child windows reside under a single parent window.

- Console-based applications do not have a graphical user interface and use a text-mode console window to interact with the user. These applications are best suited for tasks that require minimal or no user interface.

- Windows services are ideal for creating long-running applications that run in the background and do not have any user interface.

- You can create Windows services using Visual Studio's Windows Services template.

- Before a Windows service can be used, it must be installed in Windows Registry. To do this, add the Installer component to the Windows Service Application. This will allow you to install the Windows service using an installation tool such as InstallUtil.exe.

## ■ Knowledge Assessment

### Fill in the Blank

*Complete the following sentences by writing the correct word or words in the blanks provided.*

1. Use the _____ property of the ServiceInstaller class to specify a brief comment that explains the purpose of the service.

2. The _____ property of the _____ class indicates the account type under which a Windows service will run.

3. The _____ property of the EventLog class is used to specify the application name to use when writing to an event log.

4. _____ allows you to reuse existing functionality and layout for Windows Forms.

5. _____ applications are applications in which multiple child windows reside under a single parent window.

6. A(n) _____ is ideal for creating long-running applications that run in the background and do not have any user interface.

7. _____ do not have a graphical user interface and use a text-mode console window to interact with the user.

8. _____ applications provide their own window management functionality, whereas _____ applications rely on the operating system for window management.

9. A delegate can be bound to any method whose signature matches that of the _____.

10. The _____ can be bound to more than one method, allowing one-to-many notifications when an event is fired.

## Multiple Choice

*Circle the letter that corresponds to the best answer.*

1. You need to design a Windows service that cannot be paused. Which of the following options will help you accomplish this task?
   a. Set the CanPauseAndContinue property of the Windows service to False.
   b. Set the CanPauseAndContinue property of the Windows service to True.
   c. Set the CanStart property of the Windows service to True, but set the CanShutdown property to False.
   d. Do not override the OnPause and OnContinue methods in the Windows service.

2. You have developed a Windows service. You need to install this service in order to install its functionality. Which of the following options should you choose to accomplish this task?
   a. Use the Visual Studio Server Explorer.
   b. User the Services node in the Computer Management window.
   c. Use InstallUtil.exe.
   d. Use gacutil.exe.

3. You have developed a Windows service. This service need to run as a nonprivileged user in order to minimize any possible security risk. Which of the following accounts should you use for running this Windows service?
   a. LocalSystem
   b. NetworkService
   c. LocalService
   d. User (where the UserName property is set to a member of administrator role)

4. You are designing a Windows service application that contains only one Windows service. You would like this service to be started automatically when the computer is restarted. Which of the following classes should you use to specify this setting?
   a. ServiceBase
   b. ServiceInstaller
   c. ServiceProcessInstaller
   d. ServiceController

5. You need to change the display and behavior of a Windows Form so that the form can contain multiple child windows. What should you do?
   a. Set the IsMdiContainer property of the form to True.
   b. Set the MdiParent property for all the child windows.
   c. Set the MdiChild property of the form.
   d. Set the IsMdiChild property of the form.

6. You are developing a Windows Form that responds to mouse events. When the mouse moves, you need to invoke the method Form1_HandleMouse. Any code that you write should not affect any existing event-handling code. What statement should you use to attach the event handler to the event?
   a.
```
this.MouseDown = new MouseEventHandler
        (Form1_HandleMouse);
```
   b.
```
this.MouseMove = new MouseEventHandler
        (Form1_HandleMouse);
```

**c.**
```
this.MouseDown += new MouseEventHandler
        (Form1_HandleMouse);
```
**d.**
```
this.MouseMove += new MouseEventHandler
        (Form1_HandleMouse);
```

7. You are developing a Windows Form with a multiple document interface (MDI). You need to write code that arranges the child windows vertically within the client region of the MDI parent form. Which of the following statements should you use?
   **a.**
   ```
   LayoutMdi(MdiLayout.TileVertical);
   ```
   **b.**
   ```
   LayoutMdi(MdiLayout.Cascade);
   ```
   **c.**
   ```
   MdiLayout(LayoutMdi.TileVertical);
   ```
   **d.**
   ```
   MdiLayout(LayoutMdi.Cascade);
   ```

8. You are developing an application that will be run from the command line. Which of the following methods would you use for output to the command line?
   **a.** Console.Read
   **b.** Console.Write
   **c.** File.Read
   **d.** File.Write

9. You want to develop an application that displays a visual surface capable of displaying a variety of controls, such as text boxes, buttons, and menus. The application should also allow multiple child windows to reside under a single parent window. Which of the following types of application should you develop?
   **a.** Console-based application
   **b.** Windows service application
   **c.** Single document interface (SDI) application
   **d.** Multiple document interface (MDI) application

10. You are extending an existing Windows application. You would like to create a new form that derives its visual characteristics (including size, color, and some controls) from a previously created form. Which technique should you use to create the new form?
    **a.** Visual inheritance
    **b.** Visual encapsulation
    **c.** Visual abstraction
    **d.** Visual polymorphism

## ■ Competency Assessment

### Scenario 5-1: Using Visual Inheritance

You need to create a Windows Form similar to the one you created in the VisualInheritance exercise. However, this time, the requirement is that the background color of this form must match the currently selected color of the user's desktop. How would you develop such a form?

### Scenario 5-2: Handling the MouseDown Event

You are developing a game that allows users to hit a target area on a Windows Form with their mouse. You need to develop an experimental form that displays the X and Y coordinates of the location clicked by the user in the form's title bar. How should you achieve this?

## Proficiency Assessment

### Scenario 5-3: Working with Console Input

You are developing a program that manipulates text. You need to write a console-based application that accepts text from the user and converts the text to upper-case letters. What code do you need to write to meet this requirement?

### Scenario 5-4: Using the Net Utility (net.exe)

The net.exe command line utility comes installed with Windows. This utility allows you to perform various networking commands, including control of Windows services. You want to use net.exe to work with the previously created FirstService Windows service. What steps must you take in order to pause, stop, and start a Windows service using the net.exe utility?

# 6 LESSON

# Understanding Databases

| SKILLS/CONCEPTS | MTA EXAM OBJECTIVE | MTA EXAM OBJECTIVE NUMBER |
|---|---|---|
| Understanding Objects | Understand relational database management systems | 6.1 |
| Understanding Values and References | Understand database query methods. | 6.2 |
| Understanding Encapsulation | Understand database connection methods. | 6.3 |

## KEY TERMS

attribute

DataSet

database

database integrity

database management system (DBMs)

disconnected applications

element

entity-relationship diagrams (ERDs)

first normal form (1NF)

flat files

functional dependence

normalization

parameterized stored procedures

primary key

processing instructions

relational database

relational database design

second normal form (2NF)

stored procedure

Structured Query Language (SQL)

third normal form (3NF)

Extensible Markup Language (XML)

You are a software developer for the Northwind Corporation. As part of your work, you interact with and process data about customers, products, suppliers, and orders. Your work involves interacting with relational databases such as Microsoft SQL Server. However, you also work with data stored in other formats, such as flat files, XML files, and in-memory data. To be effective at your work, you need to know how to connect to various data sources and how to retrieve and update data in these sources.

## ■ Understanding Relational Database Concepts

**THE BOTTOM LINE**

A *relational database* is a collection of interrelated data based on the relational model developed by E. F. Codd. This model defines distinct data entities, their attributes, and relationships among entities.

## Understanding Databases

> A **database** is an organized collection of interrelated data that is managed as a single unit.

A database allows you to store, maintain, and retrieve important data. If a database is properly designed, it can be used by multiple applications and by multiple users. A **database management system** (DBMS), on the other hand, is software that organizes databases and provides features such as storage, data access, security, backup, etc. Examples of popular DBMSs include Microsoft SQL Server, Microsoft Access, Oracle, and MySql.

Database management systems can be implemented based on different models. Of these models, the relational model is most popular. In the relational model, data is organized into tables, each of which can have multiple rows. DBMSs based on relational models are called relational DBMSs (RDBMSs). SQL Server, Access, Oracle, and MySql are all RDBMSs.

Other database management systems are based on different models. For example, object DBMSs (ODBMSs) are based on the object model, in which data is stored as a collection of objects. In this lesson, however, we will focus solely on the more popular relational databases.

Relational DBMSs use **Structured Query Language (SQL)** to retrieve and manipulate data. Most popular relational database management systems provide some support for the standardized version of SQL, thereby allowing you to use your skills across different relational database systems.

## Understanding Relational Database Concepts

> A **relational database** organizes data in two-dimensional tables consisting of columns and rows.

A relational database organizes information into *tables*. A table is a list of rows and columns that is conceptually similar to a Microsoft Excel worksheet. A row is also called a record or tuple, and a column is sometimes called a field. The column or field specifies the type of data that will stored for each record in the table. For example, customer orders can be stored in an Orders table in which each row represents a unique order. In this table, columns such as OrderDate can be used to specify that a valid value is of the correct data type. A sample Orders table is shown in Figure 6-1.

**Figure 6-1**

An Orders table in a relational database

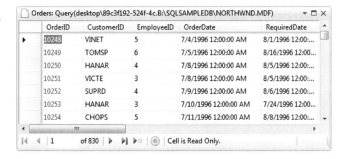

## Understanding Relational Database Design

> *Relational database design* is the process of determining the appropriate relational database structure to satisfy business requirements.

An organization's data is one of its most important assets. Thus, when you design a database, one of the guiding principles is to ensure *database integrity*. Integrity means that the data in the database is accurate and consistent at all times.

The database design process consists of the following steps:

1. **Develop a mission statement for the database:** Identifies the purpose of the database, how it will be used, and who will use it. This step sets the tone for the rest of the design process.

2. **Determine the data that needs to be stored:** Identifies all the different types of data that need to be stored in the database. Generally, this information is collected as part of the requirements analysis task via entity-relationship diagrams.

3. **Divide the data into tables and columns:** Identifies the tables and the information that you want to store in those tables.

4. **Choose primary keys:** A primary key is a column or set of columns that uniquely identifies each row of data in a table.

5. **Identify relationships:** Identifies how the data in one table is related to the data in another table. For example, for each customer in a Customers table, you may have many orders in the Orders table; this relationship is called a *one-to-many relationship*.

6. **Apply the normalization process:** Applies data normalization rules to ensure that any problems that may affect data integrity are resolved. You'll learn more about the normalization process later in this lesson.

After you've established the purpose of a database, the next set of steps (Step 2 through Step 5) can be completed as part of entity-relationship modeling. The final step of normalization can then be applied to the output from this modeling.

## Understanding Entity-Relationship Diagrams

> *Entity-relationship diagrams (ERDs)* are used to model entities, their attributes, and the relationships among entities. Entity-relationship diagrams can help you determine what data needs to be stored in a database.

Entity-relationship modeling is a process used to create the conceptual data model of a system, and entity-relationship diagrams are the graphical modeling tools for accomplishing this modeling. The basic building blocks of an ERD are entity, attribute, and relationship:

- **Entity:** An entity is a construct for a physical object or a concept. Examples include an order, a customer, an employee, and so on. An entity is generally named for the noun that it represents.

- **Attribute:** Attributes are the distinct properties of an entity. For example, for an Order entity, some useful attributes may be OrderNumber, OrderDate, ShipDate, and ShipVia. Similarly, for an Employee entity, some useful attributes may be EmployeeId, LastName, FirstName, Title, and HireDate. Every entity must have a set of uniquely identifying attributes that is known as the entity's *primary key*. For example, an OrderNumber is an attribute that uniquely identifies an order, so it is therefore a primary key for the Order entity.

- **Relationship:** A relationship is an association between entities. For example, Takes is a relationship between an Employee entity and an Order entity (i.e., Employee Takes Order).

Note that ERDs don't show single entities or single relations. For example, there may be thousands of Order entities and hundreds of Customer entities. Instead, these diagrams show entity sets and relationship sets—for instance, all the thousands of Order entities may make up one entity set. In fact, when an Order or Customer appears in an ERD, it usually refers to an entity set rather than an individual entity.

ERDs use certain design conventions. In particular:

- A rectangle represents an entity set.
- An ellipse represents an attribute.
- A diamond represents a relationship set.
- Solid lines link entity sets to relationship sets and entity sets to attributes.

Figure 6-2 shows an example ERD. In this diagram, the two entity sets are Customer and Order. Attributes associated with Customer are ID, Name, and City. Attributes associated with Order are OrderID, OrderDate, and ShipDate. Those attributes that form a primary key are under-lined. Also, as shown in the figure, the relationship between Customer and Order is Places.

**Figure 6-2**

An entity-relationship diagram

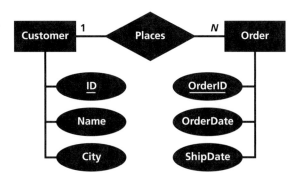

Within an ERD, a relationship can be classified as a one-to-one relationship, a one-to-many relationship, or a many-to-many relationship. In Figure 6-2, the line that connects the relationship Places with the entity set Customer is labeled "1," whereas the line between Places and the entity set Order is labeled "$N$." This is an example of a one-to-many relationship. In this relationship, one customer can place many orders, but an order can have only one customer associated with it.

## MAPPING ERDs TO A RELATIONAL DATABASE

In order to convert an ERD to a relational database, you must take following steps:

1. **Map the entities:** Start by creating a table for each entity set in the diagram. The attributes will become columns. Be sure to set the primary key attribute(s) to the primary key column(s) for the table.

2. **Map the relationship:** Next, map the one-to-many relationship by ensuring that the table on the $N$ side of the relationship contains the primary key column of the table on the 1 side of the relationship. For Figure 6-2, this can be accomplished by adding a CustomerID column in the Order table that maps to the ID column of the Customer table. In the context of the Order table, the CustomerID is also called a foreign key. By adding this column in the Order table, it is possible to answer questions such as "What are all the orders placed by a specific customer?" and "Who is the customer for a specific order?"

When mapped to a relational database, the ERD in Figure 6-2 generates the following tables:

**Customers**

| ID | NAME | CITY |
|---|---|---|
| 1001 | Jane Doe | Berlin |
| 1002 | John Doe | Tokyo |
| 1003 | Howard Steel | Sydney |

**Orders**

| ORDERID | CUSTOMERID | ORDERDATE | SHIPDATE |
|---|---|---|---|
| 101 | 1001 | 10/1/2010 | 10/7/2010 |
| 102 | 1002 | 10/5/2010 | 10/10/2010 |
| 103 | 1001 | 10/4/2010 | 10/10/2010 |

## Understanding Data Normalization

The process of data *normalization* ensures that a database design is free of any problems that could lead to loss of data integrity.

Entity-relationship analysis helps you ensure that you've identified the correct data items for your database. Then, through the process of data normalization, you apply a set of normalization rules to make sure that you have established the correct database design—that is, you check whether the columns belong to the right tables in order to ensure that your database is free of any undesirable problems.

For example, as part of entity-relationship analysis, you may come up with a Books table that has the following columns:

**Books**

| BOOKID | BOOKNAME | CATEGORYID | CATEGORYNAME |
|---|---|---|---|
| 1 | Cooking Light | 1001 | Cooking |
| 2 | Prophecy | 1002 | Mystery & Thriller |
| 3 | Shift | 1003 | Business |
| 4 | The Confession | 1002 | Mystery & Thriller |

However, this design for the Books table suffers from three problems:

- **Insert anomaly:** An insert anomaly is a situation in which you cannot insert new data into a database because of an unrelated dependency. For example, if you want your database to have a new CategoryId and CategoryName for history books, the current design will not permit that unless you first have a history book to place in that category.

- **Delete anomaly:** A delete anomaly is a situation in which the deletion of one piece of data causes unintended loss of other data. For example, if you were to delete the BookId 3 from the Books table, the very fact that you ever had a CategoryName of Business would be lost.
- **Update anomaly:** An update anomaly is a situation in which updating a single data value requires multiple rows to be updated. For example, say you decide to change the Mystery & Thriller category name to just Mystery. With the current table design, you'll have to change the category name for every book in that category. There is also a risk that if you update the category name in one row, but not the others, you'll end up having inconsistent data in the database.

Each of these problems can be fixed by following the normalization process. There are five normal forms that are used as part of this process; however, this lesson only discusses the first three, because they are all that is required in most cases.

### UNDERSTANDING THE FIRST NORMAL FORM

In order for a table to be in the first normal form (1NF), none of the columns in the table should have multiple values in the same row of data. For example, if a Customers table stores data as shown below, this table is not in 1NF because the PhoneNumber column is storing more than one value in each row.

**Customer**

| ID | FIRSTNAME | LASTNAME | PHONENUMBER |
|---|---|---|---|
| 1 | Jane | Doe | (503) 555-6874 |
| 2 | John | Doe | (509) 555-7969, (509) 555-7970 |
| 3 | Howard | Steel | (604) 555-3392, (604) 555-3393 |

For this table to be in 1NF, you would need to break the table in two:

**Customer**

| ID | FIRSTNAME | LASTNAME |
|---|---|---|
| 1 | Jane | Doe |
| 2 | John | Doe |
| 3 | Howard | Steel |

**CustomerPhones**

| ID | PHONENUMBER |
|---|---|
| 1 | (503) 555-6874 |
| 2 | (509) 555-7969 |
| 2 | (509) 555-7970 |
| 3 | (604) 555-3392 |
| 3 | (604) 555-3393 |

**TAKE NOTE***

Normalization can help you ensure a correct database design, but it cannot ensure that you have the correct data items to begin with.

**TAKE NOTE***

A general convention is to underline the name of the columns in a table that are part of the primary key.

Here, the Customers table and the CustomerPhones table are both in 1NF. Both tables have a primary key (Id in the first table and the combination of Id and PhoneNumber in the second table) that establishes a relationship between them. Given any Id for a customer, you can find all phone numbers for that customer without any confusion. On the other hand, LastName is not a primary key because a last name may have duplicate entries.

**TAKE NOTE** *

Creating repeating columns such as PhoneNumber1 and PhoneNumber2 to normalize the Customer table would not be an acceptable solution because the first normalization form does not allow such repeating columns.

## UNDERSTANDING THE SECOND NORMAL FORM

For a table to be in second normal form (2NF), it must first meet the requirements for 1NF. In addition, 2NF requires that all non-key columns are functionally dependent on the entire primary key.

In order to understand 2NF, you must first understand *functional dependence*. Let's take the example of the Customers table above. In the Customers table, the Id column is the primary key because it uniquely identifies each row. The columns FirstName and LastName are non-key columns, because they are not part of the primary key. Both FirstName and LastName are functionally dependent on Id because, given a value of Id, you can always find a value for the corresponding FirstName and LastName without any ambiguity. There is no non-key column in the Customers table that does not functionally depend on the primary key. The Customers and CustomerPhones table are therefore already in 2NF.

**TAKE NOTE** *

2NF only applies to tables that have composite primary keys (i.e., multiple columns together make up the primary key). The combined values of all fields in a composite primary key must be unique. If a table satisfies 1NF and has only a single column in its primary key, then the table also conforms to 2NF.

In contrast, consider the following table:

**Orders**

| OrderId | CustomerId | OrderDate | CustomerName |
| --- | --- | --- | --- |
| 101 | 1 | 10/1/2010 | Jane Doe |
| 102 | 2 | 10/5/2010 | John Doe |
| 103 | 1 | 10/4/2010 | Jane Doe |

Here, the OrderId and CustomerId columns together identify a unique row and therefore make up a composite primary key. However, the column OrderDate is functionally dependent only on OrderId, and the column CustomerName is dependent only on CustomerId. This violates the 2NF because the non-key columns are functionally dependent on only part of the primary key.

One possible way you could modify the Orders table to conform to 2NF is to take CustomerName out of the table and have only three columns—OrderId, CustomerId, and OrderDate—with only OrderId serving as the primary key. In this solution, both CustomerId and OrderDate are functionally dependent on OrderId and thus conform to 2NF.

## UNDERSTANDING THE THIRD NORMAL FORM

The third normal form (3NF) requires that 2NF is met and that there is no functional dependency between non-key attributes. In other words, each non-key attribute should be dependent on only the primary key and nothing else. For example, consider the following table:

**Items**

| ITEMID | SUPPLIERID | REORDERFAX |
|--------|------------|----------------|
| 101    | 100        | (514) 555-2955 |
| 102    | 11         | (514) 555-9022 |
| 103    | 525        | (313) 555-5735 |

Here, ItemId is the primary key. However, ReorderFax is a fax number for the supplier and is therefore functionally dependent on SupplierId. To satisfy the requirement of 3NF, this table should be decomposed into two tables: Items (ItemId, SupplierId) and Supplier (SupplierId, ReorderFax).

**Items**

| ITEMID | SUPPLIERID |
|--------|------------|
| 101    | 100        |
| 102    | 11         |
| 103    | 525        |

**Supplier**

| SUPPLIERID | REORDERFAX |
|------------|----------------|
| 100        | (514) 555-2955 |
| 11         | (514) 555-9022 |
| 525        | (313) 555-5735 |

**CERTIFICATION READY**
Do you understand the basics of relational database management systems?
6.1

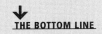

# Understanding Database Query Methods

**THE BOTTOM LINE**

Data is at the core of many business applications, and, as a developer, you will likely spend a lot of time working on data-related tasks. In this section, you will learn how to use Structured Query Language (SQL) and SQL Server-stored procedures to select, insert, update, and delete data.

SQL is the language used by most database systems to manage the information in their databases. SQL commands permit you to retrieve and update data. SQL commands also let you create and manage database objects such as tables. SQL may be thought of as a programming language for relational databases. However, SQL is declarative in nature, as opposed to the imperative nature of most common programming languages.

In SQL, you tell the database what needs to done, and it's the database's job to figure out how to do it—for example, you can tell the database to select the first 10 rows from a table. Compare this with an imperative programming language such as C#, in which you need to specify in detail how the work is to be performed. For example, you might need to create a loop that runs ten times, set up and initialize variables, move record pointers, and so on.

SQL is an ANSI (American National Standards Institute) standard, but different database vendors have implemented their own extensions to standard SQL. Microsoft SQL Server's implementation of SQL is called Transact-SQL (T-SQL).

There are two main ways to submit T-SQL to SQL Server. You can either use ad-hoc SQL statements that are executed directly, or you can use stored procedures. Stored procedures are collections of SQL statements and programming logic that are stored on the database server as named objects.

## Working with SQL Queries

SELECT, INSERT, UPDATE, and DELETE statements are the four main types of SQL statements used to manipulate SQL Server data.

Using ad-hoc SQL queries is a flexible way to work with a SQL Server database. In this portion of the lesson, you'll learn the basics about the four main types of SQL statements that help you manipulate SQL Server data:

- SELECT statements allow you to retrieve data stored in a database.
- INSERT statements allow you to add new data to a database.
- UPDATE statements allow you to modify existing data in a database.
- DELETE statements allow you to delete data from a database.

### CONNECTING TO A SQL SERVER DATABASE

You need to connect to a SQL Server database before you can manipulate any information in that database.

In this exercise, you'll learn how to work with a Microsoft SQL Server database. If you don't have access to a recent version of SQL Server, you can download SQL Server 2008 Express for free from www.microsoft.com/express/database. This exercise uses the SQL Server sample database Northwind. This database is not installed by default with SQL Server, but you can download the database file by following the instructions at www.msdn.com/en-us/library/ms143221.aspx.

Complete the following exercise to connect to and use the Northwind database with Visual Studio.

 **CONNECT TO THE NORTHWIND DATABASE**

**GET READY.** Before you begin these steps, be sure to launch Microsoft Visual Studio.

  1. Open the **Server Explorer** window. Select the **Data Connections** node, then click the **Connect to Database** button on the **Server Explorer** toolbar.

**TAKE NOTE** ★ In Visual Studio Express Edition, the Server Explorer window is called Database Explorer, and it can be opened by selecting View > Other Windows > Database Explorer.

2. In the **Add Connection** dialog box, browse to the database file for the Northwind database (northwnd.mdf), as shown in Figure 6-3.

**Figure 6-3**

Connecting to the Northwind database

3. Use Windows Authentication as the authentication mode, and click the **Test Connection** button to make sure you can connect to the database. Finally, click the **OK** button to add the connection to the database.

4. Once the connection is established, the database is available as a connection under the Data Connections node in Server Explorer. Expand the database to see the tables, stored procedures, and other database objects, as shown in Figure 6-4.

**Figure 6-4**

Accessing the Northwind database through Server Explorer

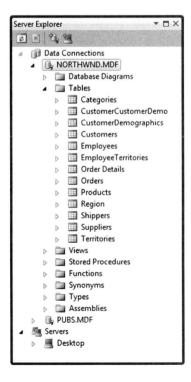

5. Right-click the **NORTHWND.MDF** node and select **Properties**. You should see the Properties window shown in Figure 6-5. In this window, notice the Connection String property. You'll use the value of this property to connect to the Northwind database from a C# application.

**Figure 6-5**

Properties window for the Northwind database

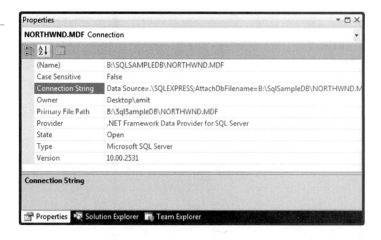

**PAUSE.** You will access data from the Northwind database in the next exercise.

## RUNNING SQL QUERIES

There are many ways to communicate with SQL Server in order to run database queries.

There are many ways in which you can send queries to a SQL Server. For example, you can use any of the following:

• Visual Studio Integrated Development Environment (IDE)
• C# application
• SQL Query Analyzer
• osql command prompt utility

Note that SQL Query Analyzer and osql command prompt utilities are tools installed with SQL Server.

 **RUN QUERIES FROM VISUAL STUDIO**

**GET READY.** To use Visual Studio IDE and C# applications to run SQL queries, perform these steps:

1. Select the **Northwind** database in the Server Explorer. Right-click the database and select **New Query**. This action opens a Query Designer and shows an Add Table dialog box. Select the **Customers** table and click **Add**. Click **Close** in the **Add Table** dialog box.

2. In the SQL pane of the Query Designer (which is the area that displays the text of the query), modify the SQL statement to the following:

   SELECT * FROM Customers

3. From the Visual Studio menu, select the **Query Designer > Execute SQL** option, or click on the **Execute SQL** button in the toolbar. The SQL statement will be sent to the SQL server for execution, and results like those in Figure 6-6 should be displayed.

**Figure 6-6**

Visual Studio Query Designer

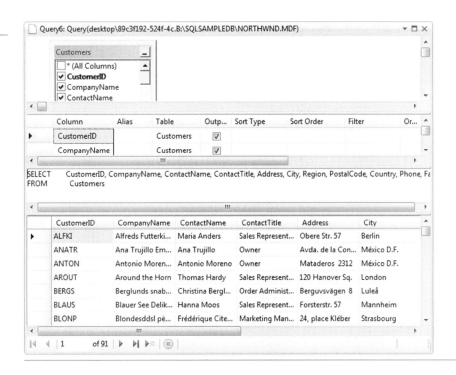

The Query Designer in Visual Studio displays up to four panes. From top to bottom, the panes are as follows:

- **Diagram pane:** This pane displays the tables involved in the query and the relationships among these tables, as well as all the columns that the tables contain.
- **Criteria pane:** The Criteria pane shows the columns that have been selected as part of the query, as well as additional sorting and filtering information.
- **SQL pane:** This pane shows the actual SQL statement that will be executed.
- **Results pane**: The Results pane shows the results (if any) after the query has been executed.

The Query Designer toolbar includes buttons that you can use to hide or show any of these four panes. For the following exercise, you need only the SQL pane and the Results pane.

 **RUN QUERIES FROM C# APPLICATION**

**GET READY.** To run queries from C# applications, do the following:

1. Create a new Windows Application project named **QueryCS**.
2. To the Windows Form, add a TextBox control, a Button control, and a DataGridView control. Set the **MultiLine** property of the TextBox to **True**. Set the **Text** property of the **Button** control to **Execute SQL**.
3. Double-click the **Button** control to generate an event handler for its Click event. Modify the event handler as shown below:

```
private void button1_Click(
    object sender, EventArgs e)
{
    if (textBox1.TextLength > 0)
    {
        SelectData(textBox1.Text);
    }
}
```

4. Add the following method to the class. Be sure to change the connection string to match the local path of the database file on your computer:

```
private void SelectData(string selectCommandText)
{
    try
    {
        // Change the connection string
        // to match with your system.
        string selectConnection =
        @"Data Source=.\SQLEXPRESS;" +
        @"AttachDbFilename=" +
        @"c:\SqlSampleDB\NORTHWND.MDF;" +
        @"Integrated Security=True;" +
        @"Connect Timeout=30;User Instance=True";
        SqlDataAdapter dataAdapter =
            new SqlDataAdapter(
             selectCommandText, selectConnection);
        DataTable table = new DataTable();
        dataAdapter.Fill(table);
        dataGridView1.DataSource = table;
    }
    catch (Exception ex)
    {
        MessageBox.Show(ex.Message);
    }
}
```

5. Add the following using directives to the code:

```
using System.Data;
    using System.Data.SqlClient;
```

Select **Debug > Start Debugging** to run the project. Enter a valid SQL query and click on the **Button** control. You should see the output shown in Figure 6-7.

**Figure 6-7**

Running queries from a C# application

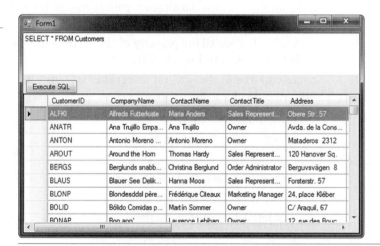

The code in this exercise implements a SelectData method that initializes a SqlDataAdapter object and uses it to populate a DataTable. The DataTable is then bound as a data source for the DataGridView component. The SqlDataAdapter object acts as a pipeline between SQL Server and the DataTable for retrieving data. The Fill method changes the data in the DataTable to match the data in the data source. The selectCommandText is used to identify the data in the data source.

## SELECTING DATA

> The SELECT statement is used to retrieve data from one or more database tables.

The SELECT statement generally takes the following form:

SELECT *list_of_fields*
FROM *list_of_tables*
WHERE *where_clause*
GROUP BY *group_by_clause*
HAVING *having_clause*
ORDER BY *order_by_clause*

Each of these lines of code in the SELECT statement is called a clause. The SELECT and FROM clauses are required, but the rest are optional. For example, here's a SQL statement that contains only the required clauses:

SELECT OrderId, CustomerId
FROM Orders

If you want to list all the fields from a table, you can also use the following shortcut instead of explicitly listing all the fields:

SELECT *
FROM Orders

In addition, you can select information from multiple tables; for example:

Select OrderId, Customers.CustomerId, ContactName
From Orders, Customers

Customers.CustomerId is known as a fully qualified name because it specifies both the table name and field name. This is necessary because both the Orders table and the Customers table include this field, so you must tell SQL Server which particular table you want to refer to.

If you run this query, you will get a lot more records than you might expect. This happens because, although you told SQL Server what tables to include, you didn't include any information on how to relate those tables. As a result, SQL Server constructs the result set to include all rows of the Customer table for every row of the Orders table. This kind of join is called a cross join, and it is not very helpful in this case.

A more useful query, of course, would match each order with the corresponding customer. The INNER JOIN keyword can help you accomplish this, as shown in the following query:

SELECT OrderID, Customers.CustomerId, ContactName
FROM Orders INNER JOIN Customers
ON Orders.CustomerId = Customers.CustomerId

This query tells SQL Server to take each row in the Orders table and match it with all rows in the Customers table in which the CustomerId of the order equals the CustomerId of the customer. Because CustomerId is unique in the Customers table, this is the same as including only a single row for each order in the result set. In this case, the result set will have as many rows as there are rows in the Orders table.

But what if you want to see only some of the rows in the table? In this situation, you can use the WHERE clause. The WHERE clause evaluates each row for a condition and decides whether to include it in the result set. For example:

TAKE NOTE *

The standard delimiter for text and dates in SQL Server is the single quotation mark.

```
SELECT *
FROM Orders
WHERE ShipCountry = 'Canada'
```

Here, the WHERE clause looks at every row in the Orders table to see whether the ShipCountry has the exact value "Canada." If it does, the row is included in the result set; if it does not, the row is not included in the result set.

You can also combine multiple conditions in a single WHERE clause. For example:

```
SELECT *
FROM Orders
WHERE (ShipCountry = 'Canada')
AND (OrderDate >= '01/01/97')
AND (OrderDate <= '01/31/97')
```

Here, the WHERE conditions filters the orders in which the ShipCountry is "Canada" and the order date is in January 1997.

By default, SQL does not guarantee the results to be in a particular order. However, you can use the ORDER BY clause to ensure that your desired data is returned in a particular order. For example, to list the orders based on their order date, you can use the following query:

```
SELECT *
FROM Orders
WHERE (ShipCountry = 'Canada')
AND (OrderDate >= '01/01/97')
AND (OrderDate <= '01/31/97')
ORDER BY OrderDate
```

You can modify the sort order by using either the keyword ASC (for ascending order) or the keyword DESC (for descending order). The default sort order is ascending. Thus, the following query lists the most recent orders at the top:

```
SELECT *
FROM Orders
WHERE (ShipCountry = 'Canada')
AND (OrderDate >= '01/01/97')
AND (OrderDate <= '01/31/97')
ORDER BY OrderDate DESC
```

It is quite common for business applications to request aggregate or summarized data. Such requirements can be addressed using the GROUP BY clause and the aggregate functions. For example, you can use the following query to find which countries you ship most of your orders to:

```
SELECT ShipCountry, COUNT(ShipCountry) AS OrderCount
FROM Orders
GROUP BY ShipCountry
ORDER BY OrderCount DESC
```

This will display the name of each country followed by the total number of orders shipped to that country. The ORDER BY clause sorts the result and places the countries with the most orders at the top of the list.

You can think of the GROUP BY clause as creating "buckets"—in this case, one for each country. As the database engine examines each record, it tosses it in the appropriate bucket. After this process is complete, the database engine counts the number of records that ended up in each bucket and outputs a row for each one. Figure 6-8 shows the start of the result set from this query.

**Figure 6-8**

Summarizing information using the GROUP BY clause

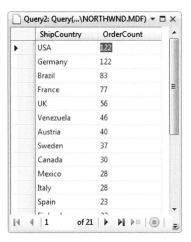

In the previous SQL statement, Count is an aggregate function—that is, it returns a result based on a group of rows. T-SQL supports a number of different aggregate functions. Some of the most common are as follows:

- **Count:** Returns the number of records
- **Sum:** Returns the total value in a given column
- **Avg:** Returns the average value in a given column
- **Min:** Returns the smallest value in a given column
- **Max:** Returns the largest value in a given column

## UPDATING DATA

The UPDATE statement is used to update information in database tables.

Another useful SQL statement is the UPDATE statement. The purpose of an UPDATE statement is to update or modify data. For example, you can update a field in a record in the Customers table using the following query:

```
UPDATE Customers
SET ContactName = 'Maria Anderson'
WHERE CustomerId = 'ALFKI'
```

In this query, the SET keyword tells SQL Server which columns to update, and the WHERE keyword tells it which rows to update. In the Customers table, CustomerId is a primary key and is uniquely identified a single row. Therefore, this UPDATE statement can update one row at most.

Note, however, that you are not limited to updating just a single record. Rather, if the WHERE clause selects multiple records, all of these records will be updated:

UPDATE Customers
SET Country = 'United States'
WHERE Country = 'USA'

You can also update more than one field at a time with an UPDATE statement, as in the following example:

UPDATE Customers
SET ContactName = 'Maria Anderson',
CITY = 'Tokyo'
WHERE CustomerId = 'ALFKI'

## INSERTING DATA

The INSERT statement is used to add one or more rows to a database table.

The INSERT statement lists the fields for the target table followed by a set of values to insert in these fields. For example, the following INSERT statement inserts a row in the Order Details table:

INSERT INTO [Order Details]
(OrderId, ProductId, UnitPrice, Quantity, Discount)
VALUES (10248, 2, 19.00, 2, 0)

Square brackets are required when the names of tables or fields contain spaces. Here, the first set of parentheses holds a column list, and the second set holds the values to insert. If a field has a default value, can be null, or is an identity field, you can leave it out of the field list, as in the following example:

INSERT INTO [Order Details]
(OrderId, ProductId, UnitPrice, Quantity)
VALUES (10249, 2, 19.00, 2)

This statement works even though no value was specified for the field Discount. Also, with this statement, you can rearrange a field list as long as you rearrange the value list to match:

INSERT INTO [Order Details]
(ProductId, OrderId, UnitPrice, Quantity)
VALUES (2, 10250, 19.00, 2)

The INSERT statement isn't limited to inserting a single record. In fact, there's a second format that inserts the results of a SELECT statement into the target table. For example, this query inserts a product from every supplier into the Products table:

INSERT INTO Products
(SupplierId, ProductName, CategoryId)
SELECT SupplierId, 'Almond', 7
FROM Suppliers

This query works by building the results of the SELECT statement and then putting each row returned by the SELECT statements into the target table. Of course, the columns still need to match properly.

## DELETING DATA

The DELETE statement is used to remove information from database tables.

The DELETE statement removes data from a table. For practice purposes and to avoid deleting data from the same database, you can copy a table using a SELECT statement, as in the following example:

```
SELECT * INTO CustomersCopy
FROM Customers
```

This statement selects all records from the Customers table and copies them to a new table named CustomersCopy.

To delete a single row of data from the CustomersCopy table, you would use the following DELETE statement:

```
DELETE FROM CustomersCopy
WHERE CustomerId = 'ALFKI'
```

Be careful, because if you omit the WHERE clause, you will delete all data from the table:

```
DELETE FROM CustomersCopy
```

## Working with Stored Procedures

A *stored procedure* is a set of SQL statements that is stored in a database. Stored procedures can be used by multiple applications.

In contrast to ad hoc queries, stored procedures are queries that are stored permanently on a SQL Server. You can think of stored procedures as the SQL equivalent of C# methods.

Stored procedures have two main benefits. First, you can use them to save complex SQL statements for future execution. Second, SQL Server compiles stored procedures so that they run faster than ad hoc queries. In this section of the lesson, you'll learn how to create and run stored procedures.

### CREATING AND RUNNING A STORED PROCEDURE

The CREATE PROCEDURE command can be used to create a new stored procedure.

You can use T-SQL's CREATE PROCEDURE keyword to create a stored procedure. You can run the CREATE PROCEDURE statement from any interface that allows you to enter and execute T-SQL.

**CREATE A STORED PROCEDURE FROM VISUAL STUDIO**

**GET READY.** To create a stored procedure from Visual Studio, perform the following actions:

1. Open **Server Explorer** and select the **Northwind** database. Right-click the **Stored Procedure** node and select the **Add New Stored Procedure** option.

2. In the stored procedure designer, replace the boilerplate text with the following code:

```
CREATE PROCEDURE GetCustomersFromFrance
AS
    SELECT * FROM Customers
    Where Country = 'France'
RETURN
```

3. Save the stored procedure. The stored procedure is now added to the database.

4. To execute the stored procedure, right-click the stored procedure in the **Server Explorer** and select **Execute**. The result from the stored procedure should be displayed in the Output window.

5. You can also execute this stored procedure from the QueryCS project that you created earlier. Here, instead of a SQL statement, just type the name of the stored procedure and click the **Execute SQL** button. The result from the stored procedure will be displayed on the Windows Form.

**TAKE NOTE***

You can use the ALTER PROCEDURE statement to modify the definition of an existing stored procedure.

## WORKING WITH PARAMETERIZED STORED PROCEDURES

*Parameterized stored procedures* allow you to pass runtime arguments to the SQL Server.

The ability to pass parameters significantly increases the power of stored procedures. The parameter values can be supplied at runtime to the stored procedures.

Say that you want to find out the total sales for a given customer in the Northwind database. In this situation, you should be able to specify the CustomerId at runtime.

 **CREATE A PARAMETERIZED STORED PROCEDURE**

**GET READY.** To create a parameterized stored procedure, take the following actions:

1. Open Server Explorer and select the **Northwind** database. Right-click the Stored Procedure node and select the **Add New Stored Procedure** option.

2. In the stored procedure designer, replace the boilerplate text with the following code:

```
CREATE PROCEDURE dbo.GetCustomerSales
    (
    @CustomerId char(5),
    @TotalSales money OUTPUT
    )
```

```
AS
    SELECT @TotalSales = SUM(Quantity * UnitPrice)
    FROM (Customers INNER JOIN Orders
    ON Customers.CustomerId = Orders.CustomerId)
    INNER JOIN [Order Details]
    ON Orders.OrderId = [Order Details].OrderId
    WHERE Customers.CustomerId = @CustomerId
RETURN
```

3. Save the stored procedure. The stored procedure is now added to the database.

In this stored procedure, both @CustomerId and @TotalSales are parameters. @CustomerId is an input parameter; you must supply a value for this parameter when you run the stored procedure. @TotalSales is an output parameter; it returns a value from the stored procedure. When you run this stored procedure from Visual Studio, you get a dialog box prompting you to enter the value for all the parameters, as shown in Figure 6-9.

**Figure 6-9**

The Run Stored Procedure dialog box prompts for the parameter values

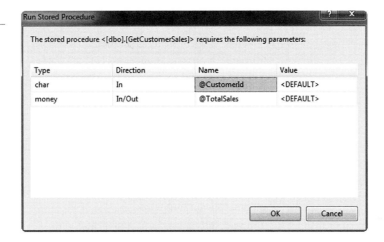

To run this stored procedure, enter ALFKI as the value for @CustomerId and enter NULL as the value for @TotalSales. When you press the OK button, the calculated value of the output parameter, @TotalSales, is displayed in the Output window.

You cannot, however, run a parameterized stored procedure from the QueryCS project, because the code there can't accept parameters.

 **RUN PARAMETERIZED STORED PROCEDURES FROM C#**

**GET READY.** To run parameterized stored procedures from C#, perform the following tasks:

1. Create a new Windows Application project named ParameterizedSP.
2. Place a **Label** control on the form and set its Text property to "Customer Id:". Place a **TextBox** control next to it and name the control as CustomerIdTextBox. Next, place a Button control and set its Name property as **GetTotalSalesButton** and the **Text** property a "Get Total Sales." Finally, place a **Label** control on the form and name it as **TotalSalesLabel**. Arrange the controls so they look similar to Figure 6-10.

3. Double-click the **Button** control to generate an event handler for its Click event. Modify the event handler as shown below:

```
private void GetTotalSalesButton_Click(
        object sender, EventArgs e)
{
    TotalSalesLabel.Text = String.Format(
        "Total Sales: {0}",
        GetTotalSales(CustomerIdTextBox.Text));
}
```

4. Add the following method to the class. Be sure to change the connection string to match the local path of the database file on your computer:

```
private double GetTotalSales(string customerId)
{
    double totalSales = -1;
    try
    {
        // Change the connection string
        // to match with your system.
        string connectionString =
        @"Data Source=.\SQLEXPRESS;" +
        @"AttachDbFilename=" +
        @"c:\SqlSampleDB\NORTHWND.MDF;" +
        @"Integrated Security=True;" +
        @"Connect Timeout=30;User Instance=True";

        SqlConnection connection =
            new SqlConnection(connectionString);
        SqlCommand command =
            connection.CreateCommand();
        command.CommandType =
            CommandType.StoredProcedure;
        command.CommandText = "GetCustomerSales";

        command.Parameters.AddWithValue(
            "@CustomerId", customerId);
        command.Parameters.AddWithValue(
            "@TotalSales", null);
        command.Parameters["@TotalSales"].DbType
            = DbType.Currency;
        command.Parameters["@TotalSales"].Direction
            = ParameterDirection.Output;

        connection.Open();
        command.ExecuteNonQuery();
```

```
                    totalSales = Double.Parse(
                          command.Parameters["@TotalSales"]
                          .Value.ToString());
                    connection.Close();
              }
              catch (Exception ex)
              {
                    MessageBox.Show(ex.Message);
              }
              return totalSales;
        }
```

**5.** Add the following using directives to the code:

using System.Data;

using System.Data.SqlClient;

Select **Debug > Start Debugging** to run the project. Enter a valid CustomerId. You should see the output shown in Figure 6-10.

**Figure 6-10**

Running parameterized stored procedures from a C# application

In the code, parameters are represented by SqlParameter objects. The code works by setting the value for the @CustomerId parameter, executing the SqlCommand object corresponding to the stored procedure, and then retrieving the Value property of the @TotalSales parameter.

**TAKE NOTE*** If you add a new row to a table with an identity column, you can use the SQL Server variable @@IDENTITY to retrieve the value of the identity column for the newly created row.

The previous code has the following lines:

connection.Open();

command.ExecuteNonQuery();

totalSales = Double.Parse(
     command.Parameters["@TotalSales"]
     .Value.ToString());

connection.Close();

Here, you first open the database connection, do what you need to do with the connection, and then close the connection. The object that holds references to the database connection uses a lot of system resources and is therefore costly to run. Accordingly, it is recommended that you close this object as soon as you are done using it. If you don't close the connection, you are creating a memory leak in the program that could impact its performance.

**CERTIFICATION READY**
Do you understand the various database query methods?
6.2

**CERTIFICATION READY**
Do you understand database connection methods?
6.3

C# also gives you a *using* statement that can help ensure that costly objects such as database connections are automatically closed when you are done with them. Here is an alternate version of the above code that makes use of the *using* statement to automatically close the database connection:

```
// disposing objects with using statement
using (connection)
{
    connection.Open();
    command.ExecuteNonQuery();
    totalSales = Double.Parse(
        command.Parameters["@TotalSales"]
        .Value.ToString());
}
```

Note that the *using* statement defines a scope for the connection object. When the code reaches the end of that scope, the connection object is automatically closed, and all resources are released.

## ■ Understanding Database Connection Methods

**THE BOTTOM LINE**

Business applications may require data in various formats. For example, you may need to work with flat files, XML files, and in-memory objects.

The .NET Framework provides classes that are optimized for working with flat files, XML files, and in-memory objects. The data stored inside flat files can be handled by using the classes in the System.IO namespace. To work with XML data, the classes in the System.Xml namespace can be used. Finally, to work with in-memory objects such as a DataSet, classes in the System.Data namespace are used. You will learn more about how to work with each of these data formats in the following sections.

### Working with Flat Files

A *flat file* is a database table that is stored inside a stand-alone disk file.

A flat file usually contains one row of data per line, and the columns are separated by delimiters such as commas or have a fixed length. The data in a flat file can be plain text or binary. These files are called "flat files" to distinguish them from more structured forms of storage, such as relational databases and XML files.

Historically, before the advent of modern databases, flat files were a popular way to store and organize information. Flat files are still useful today, although only in limited scenarios rather than as general-purpose databases. Some of the places in which flat files are used are operating system or application configuration files, when transferring data to remote systems, and when migrating data between noncompatible systems.

File-based input and output in the .NET Framework revolves around the concept of streams and backing store. A stream is a flow of raw data, and a backing store is the source or destination of the stream. A backing store might be a disk file, memory, network connection, etc. You can find classes for working with streams and backing stores in the System.IO namespace.

As previously mentioned, flat files can be in either plain-text or binary format. Text files are often organized as lines of text separated by end-of-line characters. The StreamReader and StreamWriter classes provide you with an easy way to manipulate such text files.

Binary files store their content as a sequence of bytes. Although binary files are not human-readable like text files, they are capable of storing a variety of data, such as images, sounds, video, etc. You will always need a computer program to interpret the contents of a binary file. The BinaryReader and BinaryWriter classes provide you with an easy way to manipulate binary files.

In the following exercise, you select columns from the Customers table and write them to a text file. Later, you open this text file and display its contents in the Console window.

 **READ FROM AND WRITE TO A TEXT FILE**

**GET READY.** To read from and write to a text file, do the following:

1. Create a new Console Application project named WorkingWithTextFiles.
2. Add the following code to the Program class. You will need to correct the path to your Northwind database in the code:

```
static void Main(string[] args)
{
    string myDocumentsPath =
        Environment.GetFolderPath(
        Environment.SpecialFolder.MyDocuments);
    CopyDataToTextFile(myDocumentsPath
        + @"\CustomerList.txt");
    DisplayTextFile(myDocumentsPath
        + @"\CustomerList.txt");
}
static private void CopyDataToTextFile(
    string fileName)
{
    try
    {
        // Change the connection string
        // to match with your system.
        string connectionString =
        @"Data Source=.\SQLEXPRESS;" +
        @"AttachDbFilename=" +
        @"c:\SqlSampleDB\NORTHWND.MDF;" +
        @"Integrated Security=True;" +
        @"Connect Timeout=30;User Instance=True";

        SqlConnection connection =
            new SqlConnection(connectionString);
        SqlCommand command =
            connection.CreateCommand();
```

```
                    command.CommandText =
                        "SELECT CustomerId, CompanyName,"
                        + "ContactName, Phone FROM Customers";
                using (connection)
                {
                    connection.Open();
                    SqlDataReader reader =
                        command.ExecuteReader();
                    using (StreamWriter sw =
                        new StreamWriter(fileName))
                    {
                        while (reader.Read())
                        {
                            string customerRow =
                            String.Format("{0}, {1}, {2}, {3}",
                            reader.GetValue(0),
                            reader.GetValue(1),
                            reader.GetValue(2),
                            reader.GetValue(3));
                            sw.WriteLine(customerRow);
                        }
                    }
                }
            }
            catch (Exception ex)
            {
                Console.WriteLine(ex.Message);
            }
        }
        static void DisplayTextFile(string fileName)
        {
            try
            {
                using (StreamReader sr =
                    new StreamReader(fileName))
                {
                    string line;
                    while ((line = sr.ReadLine()) != null)
                    {
                        Console.WriteLine(line);
                    }
                }
            }
```

```
                    catch (Exception ex)
                    {
                            Console.WriteLine(ex.Message);
                    }
            }
```

3. Add the following using directives to your code:

```
using System.Data.SqlClient;
    using System.IO;
```

4. Build and run the program. Check the My Documents folder for the file name CustomerList.txt and verify that the customer data has been written. Also verify the output on the Console window against the contents of the file.

The code in this exercise first opens a new StreamWriter object and calls its WriteLine method multiple times to write text to a text file. It then creates a StreamReader object to read text from the file that was just created by using the ReadLine method. When there is no data left to read, the ReadLine object returns a null value. The code uses this value to determine when to finish reading from the text file.

## Working with XML

*Extensible Markup Language (XML)* is a text-based format for representing structured data.

In XML, you can store both data and metadata (information about the data being stored). For example, the following XML represents data for two customers:

```
<?xml version="1.0" encoding="utf-8"?>
<!--Customer List-->
<Customers>
    <Customer Id="ALFKI">
        <CompanyName>Alfreds Futterkiste</CompanyName>
        <Phone>030-0074321</Phone>
    </Customer>
    <Customer Id="EASTC">
        <CompanyName>Eastern Connection</CompanyName>
        <Phone>(171) 555-0297</Phone>
    </Customer>
</Customers>
```

Even without knowing anything about XML, you can understand the contents of this file just by looking at them. XML consists of tags (contained within angle brackets) and data. Tags always appear in pairs, with each opening tag matched by a closing tag. For example, <Customers> is an opening tag, and </Customers> is the corresponding closing tag.

The first line of an XML document is the XML declaration:

```
<?xml version="1.0" encoding="utf-8"?>
```

XML tags that begin with <? are called *processing instructions*. This processing instruction tells us that the document is an XML document, conforms to the XML version 1.0 specifications, and uses the UTF-8 character set for its data elements.

An opening tag and closing tag together with their contents is called an **element**. For example, the following is a single XML element from the above document:

```
<Phone>030-0074321</Phone>
```

This bit of code defines an element with the name Phone whose value is 030-0074321. Elements can be nested, but they cannot overlap. For example, the following XML is invalid because of the overlap between the CompanyName and Phone elements:

```
<Customer Id="EASTC">
        <CompanyName>Eastern Connection<Phone>
        </Phone>(171) 555-0297</CompanyName>
    </Customer>
</Customers>
```

XML documents are hierarchical in nature. Every XML document contains a single root element that contains all the other nodes. An XML document can therefore be visualized as a tree of nodes.

Elements can contain attributes. An **attribute** is a piece of data that further describes an element. For example:

```
<Customer Id="ALFKI">
```

Here, the Customer element includes an attribute whose name is Id and whose value is ALFKI.

Finally, an XML document can contain comments. Comments start with the characters <!-- and end with the characters -->.

XML is often more complex than what is discussed in this section. However, these basics are enough for you to understand most XML documents that you'll likely run into until you start working with XML in depth.

There are many ways in which you can work with XML data. The classes that work with XML data are organized in the System.Xml namespace. This portion of the lesson focuses on the following commonly used classes:

- **XmlReader and XmlWriter:** These classes provide a fast, noncached, forward-only way to read or write XML data.
- **XmlDocument:** This class is an in-memory representation of XML data and allows navigation and editing of the XML document.

In the following exercise, you use the XmlReader class to read the XML file name Customers. xml in a sequential and forward-only manner.

 **READ FROM AN XML FILE**

**GET READY.** To read from an XML file, do the following:

1. Create a new Console Application project named WorkingWithXmlReader.
2. Add the following code to the Main method of the Program class:

```
using (XmlReader reader =
    XmlReader.Create("Customers.xml"))
{
    while (reader.Read())
    {
```

```
            if (reader.IsStartElement())
            {
                switch (reader.Name)
                {
                    case "CompanyName":
                        if (reader.Read())
                        {
                            Console.Write(
                            "Company Name: {0}, ",
                                reader.Value);
                        }
                        break;
                    case "Phone":
                        if (reader.Read())
                        {
                            Console.WriteLine(
                                "Phone: {0}", reader.Value);
                        }
                        break;
                }
            }
        }
    }
}
```

3. Next, add the following using directive to the program:

   using System.Xml;

4. Now, add a new XML file named Customers.xml to the project. Make sure the xml file contains the following data:

```xml
<?xml version="1.0" encoding="utf-8"?>
<!--Customer List-->
<Customers>
    <Customer Id="ALFKI">
        <CompanyName>Alfreds Futterkiste</CompanyName>
        <Phone>030-0074321</Phone>
    </Customer>
    <Customer Id="EASTC">
        <CompanyName>Eastern Connection</CompanyName>
        <Phone>(171) 555-0297</Phone>
    </Customer>
</Customers>
```

Build the program. Copy the Customers.xml file to the program executable folder. Run the program. You should see a list of all the company names and phone numbers.

The code in this exercise first creates a new instance of XmlReader by using the XmlReader. Create method. This will throw an exception if the file is not found. The program will terminate when the XmlReader.Read method has nothing to read. You can use properties such as Name and Value to access various portions of XML.

## Working with DataSet

> A *DataSet* is an in-memory representation of relational data.

A DataSet is an in-memory representation of relational data. Just like a database, a DataSet can have tables, relations, and data-integrity constraints such as unique constraints or foreign-key constraints. A DataSet is usually created by retrieving data from a data source such as a database. Once you have created a DataSet, you can work with all the data in the DataSet even when the link to the source data source is temporarily unavailable. When there are any changes to the data, only the in-memory copy of the data is updated. Connection to the data source is needed only when it is time to update the data source with the changes from the DataSet. DataSet is very useful for creating *disconnected applications*. Disconnected applications are applications that can continue to function without a constant connection to network resources such as databases.

All DataSet-related classes are part of the System.Data namespace. A DataSet object is created by using the DataSet class. The DataSet consists of a collection of DataTable objects. A DataTable is just like a relational database table. A DataTable object has a collection of DataColumn objects that represent the columns in the table. The rows in the DataTable are represented by the DataRow collection.

The DataAdapter acts as a bridge between the data source and the DataSet. The DataAdapter stores the data connection and data commands needed to connect to the data source. The DataAdapter also provides commands for retrieving data from the data source and commands for updating the data source with any changes.

The .NET Framework provides three DataAdapter classes to work with different type of data sources:

- The OdbcDataAdapter class is used to work with ODBC data sources.
  The OdbcDataAdapter class is part of the System.Data.Odbc namespace.
- The OleDbDataAdapter class is used to work with OLEDB data sources.
  The OleDbDataAdapter class is part of the System.Data.OleDb namespace.
- The SqlDataAdapter class is used to work with SQL Server databases.
  The SQLDataAdapter class is part of the System.Data.SqlClient namespace.

> **TAKE NOTE***
>
> You can also connect to a SQL Server database by using the OdbcAdapter and OleDbAdapter classes. However, the SQLDataAdapter class is optimized for SQL Server. Therefore, when working with SQL Server, it is preferable to use the SQLDataAdapter class.

In a typical application that creates and updates a DataSet, you will need to carry out the following steps:

1. Build and fill each DataTable in the DataSet with data from the data source by using a DataAdapter.

2. Change the data in the individual DataTable objects by adding, updating, or deleting DataRow objects.

3. Invoke the AcceptChanges method on the dataset. This method connects to the original data sources and updates them with all the changes made to the DataSet since it was loaded or since the last time AcceptChanges was called. Alternatively, you can call the RejectChanges method to cancel all the changes that were made to the DataSet since it was loaded or since the last time AcceptChanges was called.

In the following exercise, you use the classes discussed so far to read data from the SQL Server's Northwind database into a DataSet and then iterate over the Customer table to display the order numbers for each customer.

 **READ FROM AN IN-MEMORY DATASET OBJECT**

**GET READY.** To read from an in-memory DataSet Object, do the following:

1. Create a new Console Application project named WorkingWithDataSet.
2. Replace the code in the Program class with the following code. Be sure to change the connection string to match the local path of the database file on your computer:

```
static void Main(string[] args)
{
    WorkingWithDataSet();
}
static void WorkingWithDataSet()
{
    string cString = @"Data Source=.\SQLEXPRESS;"
    + @"AttachDbFilename=B:\SqlSampleDB\NORTHWND.MDF;"
    + "Integrated Security=True;"
    + "Connect Timeout=30;User Instance=True";
    SqlConnection northwindConnection =
        new SqlConnection(cString);
    string customerCommandText =
        "SELECT * FROM Customers";
    SqlDataAdapter customerAdapter =
        new SqlDataAdapter(
        customerCommandText, northwindConnection);
    string ordersCommandText =
        "SELECT * FROM Orders";
    SqlDataAdapter ordersAdapter =
        new SqlDataAdapter(
            ordersCommandText, northwindConnection);
```

```
DataSet customerOrders = new DataSet();
customerAdapter.Fill(
    customerOrders, "Customers");
ordersAdapter.Fill(
    customerOrders, "Orders");

DataRelation relation =
    customerOrders.Relations.Add("CustomerOrders",
    customerOrders.Tables["Customers"]
        .Columns["CustomerID"],
    customerOrders.Tables["Orders"]
        .Columns["CustomerID"]);
foreach (DataRow customerRow in
    customerOrders.Tables["Customers"].Rows)
{
    Console.WriteLine(customerRow["CustomerID"]);
    foreach (DataRow orderRow in
        customerRow.GetChildRows(relation))
        Console.WriteLine("\t" +
            orderRow["OrderID"]);
}
    Console.WriteLine(
        "Press any key to continue . . .");
    Console.ReadKey();
}
```

3. Add the following using directive to the program:

   ```
   using System.Data;
   using System.Data.SqlClient;
   ```

4. Select **Project > Set as Startup Project** to set the project as the startup project for the solution.

5. Select **Debug > Start Debugging** (or press **F5**) to run the program. Notice that the console window lists all the customers from the Customers table. Each CustomerID is followed by the OrderID corresponding to that customer.

**CERTIFICATION READY**
Do you understand the various database connection methods?
6.3

The code in this exercise first creates a DataSet with two DataTable objects, Customers and Orders. The DataSet also creates a DataRelation object that establishes the relationship between the Customers and the Orders table on the CustomerID column. This relationship allows you to call the GetChildRow method on a customer row to retrieve the order rows corresponding to each customer.

**TAKE NOTE***

A DataSet can read and write data as XML documents. To write data as XML, use the WriteXml method of the DataSet class. To read XML document data, use the ReadXml method of the DataSet class.

## SKILL SUMMARY

**IN THIS LESSON, YOU LEARNED THE FOLLOWING:**

- A relational database organizes information into tables. A table is a list of rows and columns.

- Relational database design is the process of determining the appropriate relational database structure to satisfy the business requirements.

- Entity-relationship diagrams are used to model the entities, their attributes, and the relationships among entities. The entity-relationship diagrams can help you in determine what data needs to be stored in a database.

- The process of data normalization ensures that a database design is free of any problems that could lead to loss of data integrity. Most design issues can be resolved by ensuring that the tables satisfy the requirements of the third normal form.

- The Structured Query Language (SQL) provides statements such as SELECT, INSERT, UPDATE, and DELETE to work with relational data.

- A stored procedure is a set of SQL statements that is stored in a database. Stored procedures can be used by multiple applications.

- The XmlReader and XmlWriter classes provide a fast, noncached, forward-only way to read or write XML data. The XmlDocument class is an in-memory representation of XML data and allows navigation and editing of the XML document.

- The DataSet class represents an in-memory representation of relational data. The DataAdapter class acts as a bridge between the data source and the DataSet. The DataAdapter stores the data connection and data commands needed to connect to the data source.

# Knowledge Assessment

## Fill in the Blank

*Complete the following sentences by writing the correct word or words in the blanks provided.*

1. In order for a table to be in the _____, none of the columns should have multiple values in the same row of data.

2. The _____ requires that all non-key columns are functionally dependent on the entire primary key.

3. The _____ requires that there is no functional dependency among non-key attributes.

4. The basic building blocks for an entity-relationship diagram are _____, _____, and _____.

5. The _____ clause in a SELECT statement evaluates each row for a condition and decides whether to include it in the result set.

6. The object used with the *using* statement must implement the _____ interface.

7. T-SQL's _____ statement can be used to create a stored procedure.

8. In the process of _____, you apply a set of rules to ensure that your database design helps with data integrity and ease of maintenance in the future.

9. You find classes for working with streams and backing stores in the _____ namespace.

10. The _____ format is a hierarchical data representation format.

## Multiple Choice

*Circle the letter that corresponds to the best answer.*

1. Your application needs to store the product image out to a disk file. You'd like to minimize the size of this disk file. Which of the following objects should you use to write the file?
   a. FileStream
   b. StreamWriter
   c. BinaryWriter
   d. XmlWriter

2. Your C# program needs to return the total number of customers in a database. The program will be used several times a day. What is the fastest way to return this information from your program?
   a. Write a SQL query and use the SqlCommand.ExecuteScalar method to execute the query.
   b. Create a stored procedure to return the total number of customers, then use the SqlCommand.ExecuteScalar method to execute the stored procedure.
   c. Write a SQL query and use the SqlDataAdapter.Fill method to execute the query.
   d. Create a stored procedure to return the total number of customers, then use the SqlDataAdapter.Fill method to execute the stored procedure.

3. You need to modify the records in a Products table by marking certain products as Discontinued. However, you need to do this only when the UnitsInStock and UnitsOnOrder are both zero. Which of the following SQL statements should you use?
   a. INSERT
   b. SELECT
   c. UPDATE
   d. DELETE

4. You need to update the Region fields for customers in Japan. You write the following SQL UPDATE statement:

   UPDATE Customers

   SET Region = 'EastAsia'

   You test the query on a test database and find that more records were affected than you expected. You need to correct the SQL statement. What should you do?
   a. Add a WHERE clause to the UPDATE statement.
   b. Add an additional SET clause to the UPDATE statement.
   c. Add a GROUP BY clause to the UPDATE statement.
   d. Add a HAVING clause to the UPDATE statement.

5. You are developing an application that needs to retrieve a list of customers from a SQL Server database. The application should move through the list sequentially once, processing each customer's record. Which of the following classes should you use to hold the customer list in order to achieve maximum performance?
   a. DataSet
   b. DataTable
   c. DataView
   d. SqlDataReader

6. The application you are developing needs to read data from a flat file that include items such as a five-digit integer key, followed by a 20-character customer name, followed by two date and time fields. Which of the following classes should you use?
   a. FileStream
   b. StreamReader
   c. BinaryReader
   d. DataReader

7. You are developing an application that will need to copy data from a SQL Server view to a DataSet. You name the DataSet object dsData. Which of the following methods should you use to copy the data?
   a. Fill
   b. InsertCommand
   c. SelectCommand
   d. Update

8. You are developing an application that manages customers and their orders. Which of the following situations is not a good candidate for implementation with stored procedures in your application?
   a. Retrieving the list of all customers in the database
   b. Retrieving the list of all orders for particular customers
   c. Inserting a new order into the Orders table
   d. Ad hoc querying by the database administrator

9. Your application connects to a SQL Server database that contains a table called Employees with the following columns:

   EmployeeID (int, identity)

   EmployeeType (char(1))

   EmployeeDate (datetime)

   You need to write a query that deletes all rows from the table where the EmployeeType value is either C or T. You do not want to delete any other rows. Which statement should you use?

   a. `DELETE FROM Employees`
      `WHERE EmployeeType LIKE '[CT]'`
   b. `DELETE FROM Employees`
      `WHERE EmployeeType LIKE '[C-T]'`
   c. `DELETE FROM Employees`
      `WHERE EmployeeType LIKE 'C' OR 'T'`
   d. `DELETE * FROM Employees`
      `WHERE EmployeeType IN ('C', 'T')`

10. Your application includes a SqlDataAdapter object named sqlDataAdapter that connects to the Employees table. Based on this SQLDataAdapter, your application also includes a DataSet object dsEmployees. What line of code should you use to load the data from the database into the DataSet object?
    a. `dsEmployees = sqlDataAdapter.Fill("Employees");`
    b. `sqlDataAdapter.Fill("dsEmployees", "Employees");`
    c. `sqlDataAdapter.Fill(dsEmployees);`
    d. `sqlDataAdapter.Fill(dsEmployees, "Employees");`

## Competency Assessment

### Scenario 6-1: Creating an Entity-Relationship Diagram

A company has a number of employees, and each employee may be assigned to one or more projects. In addition, each project can have one or more employees working on it. Draw an entity-relationship diagram for this situation.

### Scenario 6-2: Creating a Stored Procedure

You often need to generate a list of customers from a given country. Therefore, you decide to create a stored procedure that accepts the name of country as a parameter and returns all the customers from that country. How would you go about doing this?

## Proficiency Assessment

### Scenario 6-3: Normalizing Tables

You are converting an entity-relationship diagram into tables. You come up with the following table design:

**Books**

| BookId | BookName | CategoryId | CategoryName |
|--------|-----------|------------|------------------|
| 1 | Cooking Light | 1001 | Cooking |
| 2 | Prophecy | 1002 | Mystery & Thriller |
| 3 | Shift | 1003 | Business |
| 4 | The Confession | 1002 | Mystery & Thriller |

You need to apply normalization rules to ensure data integrity. How would you ensure that the Books table is in the third normal form?

### Scenario 6-4: Creating and Handling Events

You are working on an application that requires you to save customer information from the Customers table of the Northwind database into an XML file. This XML file will be used for various data-integration tasks. You need to make sure that the root node of the XML is called Customers. The root node will then have a Customer node for each customer in the Customers table. How should you accomplish this task?

| OBJECTIVE DOMAIN | SKILL NUMBER | LESSON NUMBER |
| --- | --- | --- |
| **Understanding Core Programming** | | |
| Understand computer storage and data types. | 1.1 | 1, 2 |
| Understand computer decision structures. | 1.2 | 1 |
| Identify the appropriate method for handling repetition. | 1.3 | 1 |
| Understand error handling. | 1.4 | 1 |
| **Understanding Object-Oriented Programming** | | |
| Understand the fundamentals of classes. | 2.1 | 2 |
| Understand inheritance. | 2.2 | 2 |
| Understand polymorphism. | 2.3 | 2 |
| Understand encapsulation. | 2.4 | 2 |
| **Understanding General Software Development** | | |
| Understand application lifecycle management. | 3.1 | 3 |
| Interpret application specifications. | 3.2 | |
| Understand algorithms and data structures. | 3.3 | 3 |
| **Understanding Web Applications** | | |
| Understand Web page development. | 4.1 | 4 |
| Understand Microsoft ASP.NET Web application development. | 4.2 | 4 |
| Understand Web hosting. | 4.3 | 4 |
| Understand Web services. | 4.4 | 4 |
| **Understanding Desktop Applications** | | |
| Understand Windows Forms applications. | 5.1 | 5 |
| Understand console-based applications. | 5.2 | 5 |
| Understand Windows services. | 5.3 | 5 |
| **Understanding Databases** | | |
| Understand relational database query methods. | 6.1 | 6 |
| Understand database query methods. | 6.2 | 6 |
| Understand database connection methods. | 6.3 | 6 |

# Notes

# Notes

# Notes

# Notes

# Notes

# Notes

# Notes

# Notes

# Notes